Collecting and Investing Strategies
for Walking Liberty Half Dollars

By: Jeff Ambio

Collecting and Investing Strategies for Walking Liberty Half Dollars
By: Jeff Ambio

Copyright © 2008
ZYRUS PRESS INC.

Published by:
ZYRUS PRESS INC.
PO Box 17810, Irvine, CA 92623
Tel: (888) 622-7823 / Fax: (800) 215-9694
www.zyruspress.com
ISBN# 978-1-933990-17-0 (paperback)

Coin images reproduced within this work with permission from
Bowers and Merena.

Cover art by Bryan D. Stoughton.

Dedication

To my son Tristan Drew. May God be with you always and guide you along the path of a successful and rewarding life. Love always – Dad.

About the Author

Jeff Ambio holds a Bachelor of Arts in History from Cornell University and a Masters of Business Administration from Pepperdine University. Upon graduating from Cornell in 1998, Ambio decided to turn a life-long passion for coin collecting into a full-time career. Over the past 10 years, his career has developed into a successful and rewarding profession. Today, few other professional numismatists can lay claim to so prolific a career in so short a period of time. Ambio's numismatic resume reads like a directory of America's most prestigious rare coin auction houses and dealerships, and his writings provide collectors, investors and even other dealers with many of the tools and knowledge that they need to build significant collections and conduct successful businesses.

Ambio's first position as a professional numismatist was as a Cataloger and, later, Catalog Production Manager for the U.S. coin division of Heritage Numismatic Auctions (now Heritage Auction Galleries) in Dallas, Texas. During his tenure with Heritage, Jeff handled thousands of rare coins, produced dozens of catalogs and designed many of the marketing pieces published by the firm.

In 2003 and 2004, Ambio served as a Cataloger for Superior Galleries of Beverly Hills. He relocated to California in 2004 and accepted the position of Director of Numismatics for Bowers and Merena Auctions of Irvine. Jeff also served as Vice President of Numismatics for Rare Coin Wholesalers of Dana Point, California.

In addition to extensive cataloging and marketing experience, Jeff is a widely read numismatic author. His writings and articles are credited with ground-breaking work in the field and have appeared in numerous publications, including *Rare Coin Investment Trends*, *The Gobrecht Journal*, *Numismatic News* and *Coin World*. Ambio is also the author of the book *Collecting & Investing Strategies for United States Gold Coins* and editor of David W. Akers' classic book, *A Handbook of 20th-Century United States Gold Coins: 1907-1933*.

Early in his career, Ambio's achievements as a numismatist were honored with a scholarship to attend the American Numismatic Association (ANA) Summer Seminar. In 2007, Jeff came full circle, this time returning to the ANA Summer Seminar as an instructor and originator of the course "Attributing United States Coins." In addition to several local and regional organizations, Jeff is a member of the ANA and the NLG.

In 2007, Ambio returned to his lakeside home in Texas, where he now works as a technical and marketing consultant for rare coin auction houses, dealerships and brokerage firms across the United States. Shortly after relocating to Texas, Jeff graduated from the Texas Auction Academy and founded his own rare coin dealership, Ambio Rare Coins (ARC). Jeff is the loving husband of Misty Renee and the proud father of one son, Tristan Drew. In his spare time, he enjoys fishing and studying European military history.

Foreword

Forty-plus years ago, Walking Liberty Half Dollars were still plentiful in circulation. The patient collector could acquire a complete set of dates and mintmarks simply by searching through bank-wrapped rolls of half dollars. Upgrades were relatively inexpensive and the collector who had neither the luck nor the patience to find any of the scarce dates could walk into any coin shop and buy them with ease. The later dates were no problem; high grade examples were all over the place.

Back then, few people possessed the sophistication, the knowledge, the foresight, or the funds to put aside the best quality Walking Liberty Half Dollars. While most collectors followed the maxim "Buy the best quality you can afford," they usually did not purchase the BEST quality coins. No one knew that the best quality coins would be so valuable in the future.

Today, conditions have changed dramatically. Gem condition Walking Liberty Half Dollars routinely sell for tens of thousands of dollars. Even the high price of silver caused the cost of a circulated set to more than double over the past two years. Additionally, many baby boomers who grew up with Walking Liberty Half Dollars now have substantial incomes or discretionary income with which to purchase the best quality coins.

Because of the high cost of gem quality "Walkers" and the potential for costly mistakes, it becomes imperative for collectors to arm themselves with as much relevant information as possible. Collectors these days need answers to myriad questions, such as: Is it possible to find a fully struck 1918-S? Do all "slab" brands bring the same amount of money at auction? How much does eye appeal affect the value of my coins? Jeff Ambio answers all these questions and more, providing you the protection and ammunition you need to go out and buy with confidence.

Jeff Ambio is a rising star in numismatics. I met Jeff for the first time at a Long Beach convention in late 1999. He impressed me then like few people ever have in the coin business. He is bright, intelligent, well-spoken, witty, a sponge for information, a superb writer and researcher, and, to top it all off, he's a genuinely nice guy. Today, you get to "meet" him in person through his writing. I hope that someday, as did I, you have the pleasure of meeting him in person.

Ron Guth
Professional Numismatist &
President
Professional Coin Grading Service (PCGS)
Newport Beach, California
April 25th, 2008

Preface

This book had its origins in 2001 when Professional Coin Grading Service (PCGS) – one of the two leading third-party certification services in the rare coin market of the 21st century – launched the Set Registry concept for United States coins. Through the PCGS Set Registry, collectors can track their progress as they build a collection, the ultimate goal being to compete against other collectors for the honor of having the highest-ranked collection of one or more types of United States coins. The Set Registry concept has resulted in increased demand and prices for many types and individual issues. It has also provided a greater appreciation for the high-grade rarity of many issues in the United States coinage family. According to current PCGS President Ron Guth, the Set Registry is, *"...one of the four legs of the PCGS formula for success."*

The PCGS Set Registry, as well as the NGC Registry that was launched a short while later, have had the most profound effect on the demand and prices for the more popular series in U.S. numismatics. These include Mercury Dimes, Standing Liberty Quarters, Morgan Dollars and, most importantly for this book, Walking Liberty Half Dollars. Thanks to the Set Registry concept, the market for Walking Liberty Half Dollars was revolutionized almost overnight. More and more collectors started to take notice of the rarity of even common-date Walking Liberty Half Dollars in the highest Mint State grades, and prices rose sharply to reflect a marked increase in demand at those levels. Numerous issues were affected by this phenomenon, one of which is the 1935. This is a relatively plentiful issue in lower Mint State grades, but it is conditionally rare as a Superb Gem. A PCGS MS-67 sold for just $1,650 when offered at auction in January of 1996. In November of 2002, only about one year after the launch of the PCGS Set Registry, another 1935 Half Dollar certified MS-67 at PCGS realized $3,105 at auction. A nearly 100% price increase for this issue in MS-67 during only a six-year period can only be explained by a sharp increase in demand due to the launch of the Set Registry program.

With more collectors entering the market for Walking Liberty Half Dollars and the dynamic of that market evolving and changing at a near-exponential rate, it became obvious that this popular 20th century series was in need of reassessment. I received further confirmation of this need during the six-year period from 2002 to 2007. During that time I served as a primary cataloger and researcher at several leading rare coin auction houses and was given the opportunity to handle several Walking Liberty Half Dollar Registry Sets that were being offered for sale. The formation and dispersal of these sets brought into the mainstream market many simply extraordinary Walking Liberty Half Dollars the existence of which was unknown prior to 2001, save for perhaps among a few specialized collectors and dealers. The emergence of these coins has allowed the market to reevaluate the high-grade rarity of many issues in the Walking Liberty Half Dollar series, as well as increase our understanding of the striking and surface characteristics of these coins.

This book is certainly not the first scholarly study of the Walking Liberty Half Dollar series. Two earlier works stand out as having made particularly important contributions to our understanding of the Walking Liberty Half Dollar series. Anthony Swiatek, former president of the American Numismatic Association (ANA) and a recognized expert on many segments of the U.S. rare coin market, published a work on Walking Liberty Half

Dollars in 1983 that I still believe is required reading for any serious student of this series. The same must also be said for Bruce Fox's 1993 book *The Complete Guide to Walking Liberty Half Dollars*.

Swiatek's work on this series, however, was published prior to the founding of PCGS and NGC. In other words, he carried out his research at a time when grading standards were much less strict than they are in the market of the early 21st century. Additionally, Swiatek did not have the benefit of PCGS and NGC population reports – powerful tools for determining the relative rarity between different issues in a given series as well as the grade distribution among surviving examples of a single issue. Fox, on the other hand, wrote his indispensable reference on Walking Liberty Half Dollars before PCGS introduced the Set Registry concept. The handicaps that these authors labored under, as well as the significance and lasting impact of their work, highlights their accomplishments as numismatic scholars.

It has been a quarter of a century since publication of Swiatek's work on Walking Liberty Half Dollars, and Fox's book has been in print for 15 years. Both are becoming increasingly difficult to find. Additionally, neither work takes into consideration current third-party grading standards, up-to-date population data from PCGS and NGC, prices realized for significant Registry Sets and individual coins that have been dispersed through auction from 2000-2007 or a host of other information that is indispensable for the Walking Liberty Half Dollar collector operating in the U.S. rare coin market of the 21st century.

My goal in writing this book is to reevaluate the Walking Liberty Half Dollar series in light of the profound changes that have taken place in the market for these coins during the past 15-25 years. Whether you are in the market for a single Walking Liberty Half Dollar to use as a type coin, or you plan on spending many years assembling the finest collection of this series that money can buy, it is my sincere hope that you will find the information presented in the following pages invaluable in achieving your collecting goals. If you have yet to discover the joys associated with collecting Walking Liberty Half Dollars, may this book serve as your passport as you begin to explore one of the most beautiful and challenging coins ever struck in the United States Mint.

Jeff Ambio
Texas, June 2008

Acknowledgements

Several firms and individuals were instrumental in the publication of this book. I owe a special debt of gratitude to my publisher Bart Crane and the entire team at Zyrus Press. Bart has been overly generous with his time and resources in the production of this book. Without his expertise and dedication, this project would never have been possible. Thank you.

I would also like to acknowledge Elaine Dinges, Ceilia Mullins and everyone at Bowers and Merena Auctions for furnishing many of the Walking Liberty Half Dollar images used in this book. Ceilia, in particular, spent many hours gathering these images and ensuring that they were in print-ready format. Additional Walking Liberty Half Dollar images were graciously provided by Steven L. Contursi and Rare Coin Wholesalers. Thank you, Steve, for your continued support.

Finally, I would like to recognize Ron Guth, President of Professional Coin Grading Service (PCGS). As a close friend and wise counsel on many aspects of the rare coin market, Ron has been an invaluable resource in my development as a professional numismatic cataloger, author and researcher. He has always given freely of his time and knowledge, most recently by agreeing to write the Foreword to this book. Thank you, Ron, for playing such an integral part in my numismatic career.

Table of Contents

Introduction

The bulk of this book is devoted to a detailed analysis of every business strike and proof issue in the Walking Liberty Half Dollar series of 1916-1947. I encourage you, however, to read the introductory chapters before delving into the date and mintmark analyses. The present chapter is invaluable to discerning my methodology on researching and writing this book, as well as understanding the parameters of this study and how to interpret the information that I have gathered on this important series.

In Chapter 1: Popular Collecting and Investing Strategies for Walking Liberty Half Dollars, I suggest several methods through which you can build a meaningful collection and/or investment portfolio comprised either in whole or in part of Walking Liberty Half Dollars. Chapter 2: Considerations for Buying Walking Liberty Half Dollars outlines several key factors governing the nature of the market in which these coins trade. Particularly important aspects of that chapter are observations on third-party certification and suggestions on how and where to acquire Walking Liberty Half Dollars. Finally, Chapter 3: A Brief History of the Walking Liberty Half Dollar Series details the birth of this series, the evolution of the design throughout its production and broad themes affecting yearly mintages and/or distribution of the coins.

Chapter 4 begins the main issue-by-issue Date & Mintmark Analysis of the Walking Liberty Half Dollar series. The information presented on each business strike and proof issue is based on the thousands of Walking Liberty Half Dollars that I have cataloged for auction, bought and sold or otherwise handled over the course of 10 years as a professional numismatist. Other books such as *A Guide Book of United States Coins*, 61st Edition by R.S. Yeoman, *The Complete Guide to Walking Liberty Half Dollars* by Bruce Fox and *Walter Breen's Complete Encyclopedia of U.S. and Colonial Coins* were consulted only to verify facts such as mintage figures, attributions for significant die varieties, etc.

I have limited my discussion of the business strike issues in this series to Mint State coins. While this decision may come as a shock or disappointment to some readers, realize that it has been made after serious consideration and thorough reflection. The U.S. rare coin market of the 21st century is fixated on technical quality. With the exception of costly key-date issues, some of which are unknown in Mint State anyway, the lion's share of the money that changes hands in any given year of numismatic trading concerns coins that grade MS-60/Proof-60 or finer. These are certainly the levels at which the typical numismatic investor is likely to spend the majority of his or her money.

Conscious of current and future demand for the coins that they buy, more and more collectors are also coming to the realization that they have to acquire the finest in technical quality that they can afford in order to best protect their investment in numismatics. In fact, ever-increasing prices for rare and desirable United States coins have largely forced the transformation of the pure collector into a collector-investor. This new breed of numismatist is still a collector at heart who is drawn to coins because of their historical significance, artistic beauty or some other innate quality that the coins possess. Unlike the pure collector, however, the collector-investor views their collection not so much as a family heirloom to pass on to children and grandchildren, but as an integral part of a well-rounded investment portfolio. Whether this portfolio is meant to provide short-term tax benefits or long-term security, collector-investors embark on their pursuit of rare coins with the intention of selling all or part of their collection within their lifetime.

The Walking Liberty Half Dollar series is one of several in the U.S. coinage family for which Mint State and unimpaired proof coins have nearly monopolized collector and investor interest. The reason for this is not because circulated Walking Liberty Half Dollars are unattractive coins. The design actually held up very well in commercial channels – much more so, I believe, than that of some other 20th century coin types such as the Franklin Half Dollar and the Peace Dollar – and even low-grade examples in Good and VG are relatively attractive. Rather, Walking Liberty Half Dollars are so widely pursued in Mint State and unimpaired proof grades because the type is readily accessible at those levels. Even in MS-65, examples of most 1940s issues can be obtained for only a few hundred dollars, if not in the $100-$200 price range. And even many early, scarcer issues in this series are quite affordable in MS-63 and MS-64. Finally, all proof issues in the Walking Liberty Half Dollar series were produced in more-or-less sizeable numbers, and many examples have survived in Choice, Gem and even Superb Gem quality. The key-date proof 1936 certainly commands a significant premium, but it is not really a rare issue in an absolute sense. In fact, your only real impediment to acquiring an attractive proof 1936 should be your ability to pay for the coin.

Within the analysis that I have provided for each business strike and proof issue in the Walking Liberty Half Dollar series, you will find first and foremost a statement of the number of coins struck. The Walking Liberty Half Dollar series was not subject to widespread exportation or melting like other U.S. coin types such as the Seated Dollar, Morgan Dollar and Saint-Gaudens Double Eagle. As such, mintage figures are a fairly accurate indicator of assessing relative rarity in Mint State for many issues in the Walking Liberty Half Dollar series.

I have undertaken what I believe to be the first serious attempt to rank the business strike and proof issues in this series in terms of overall rarity in Mint State/Proof and rarity in high grades (MS-65/Proof-65 or finer). The results of this study are located at the beginning of each date and mintmark analysis, as well as in the appendices at the end of this book. For each issue, I have provided its rankings within the context of the entire Walking Liberty Half Dollar series as well as the specific portion of the series to which it belongs. In my opinion, the Walking Liberty Half Dollar series can be viewed and analyzed as three distinct subseries based on the manner in which the issues were distributed and/or saved. These subseries are: early-date issues from 1916-1933; middle-date issues from 1934-1940; and late-date issues from 1941-1947. Many collectors have even chosen to build partial sets of Walking Liberty Half Dollars based on the divisions that define these subseries.

This book is not an attribution guide, although you will find a subsection entitled Important Varieties near the beginning of each date and mintmark analysis. I have chosen to define the term "important" in this context as only those varieties that are recognized by the third-party grading services Professional Coin Grading Service (PCGS) and Numismatic

Guaranty Corporation (NGC), carry a significant premium over regular examples of their respective issues and/or are visually dramatic. If you are seeking a more comprehensive study of Walking Liberty Half Dollar varieties, I highly recommend, among other books, *The Complete Guide to Walking Liberty Half Dollars* by Bruce Fox, *Cherrypickers' Guide to Rare Die Varieties of United States Coins*, Fourth Edition, Volume II by Bill Fivaz and J.T. Stanton and *Walter Breen's Complete Encyclopedia of United States and Colonial Coins*.

After a brief introductory paragraph entitled General Comments, you will find my observations concerning Strike, Luster (Finish for the Proof issues), Surfaces, Toning and Eye Appeal for the issue. In each of these characteristics, I consider my observations as fact for the majority of examples that I have examined for each issue in this series. Most Walking Liberty Half Dollar issues were produced in sizeable numbers, and there is sometimes considerable variation between coins struck from different die pairs, during different press runs from the same die pair or even during the same press run. Additionally, and although I have handled thousands of Walking Liberty Half Dollars during the ten-year period from 1999-2008, no one numismatist can ever hope to see every single example of a given issue. This is particularly true of common issues with thousands of Mint State or proof examples known, of which there are many in the Walking Liberty Half Dollar series. Please accept my observations as indicative of the striking and other characteristics for the majority of examples of a given issue that you are likely to encounter in the numismatic market.

After detailing the physical characteristics of the issue, each date and mintmark analysis provides a list of Significant Examples. This list is not a Condition Census. I have not attempted a Condition Census for the Walking Liberty Half Dollar series for two reasons. First, many issues in this series have sizeable populations of coins even at those grade levels at which they top out at in the *PCGS Population Report* and *NGC Census*. Determining the five or six-finest examples of, say, the 21 MS-68s that PCGS reports for the 1940 (December/2007) is an exercise that is likely to bring out as many different opinions as there are collectors, investors and dealers in the rare coin market. Second, it is becoming increasingly difficult to keep track of individual coins in today's market as coins are upgraded due to changing grading standards, crossed from an NGC holder to a PCGS holder (or vice versa) at the same grade level, dipped to remove unsightly toning or submitted to Numismatic Conservation Service (NCS, a division of NGC) to remove spots or other harmful elements on the surfaces. These comments are not meant to disparage the practice of dipping or the excellent services that NCS provides – they are simply a statement of widely accepted practices that form the basis of how coins are conserved and traded in the U.S. rare coin market.

The sections on significant examples that I have provided for each issue, therefore, are merely a listing of some of the finest-known examples that have passed through auction during the final years of the 20th and, to a much greater extent, the early years of the 21st centuries. Every effort has been made to cross-reference auction records in order to determine multiple auction appearances for the same coin. I believe that I have largely succeeded in this endeavor, although some duplication of the same coin(s) may be present within an issue's significant examples list due to the aforementioned difficulties in tracing individual coins in today's market. Poor-quality photos in auction catalogs can also cause difficulties in this regard by obscuring small, yet important pedigree markers. Finally, some coins might be missing from an issue's significant examples list either because I was not aware of the coin's existence at the time this book went to print or because the coin has largely traded outside of auction. Direct sales between dealers and from dealers to collectors/investors are very difficult to track because they are often private and known only to the parties involved. The lists of significant examples, therefore, do not include dealer and collector intermediaries that might have owned the coin before or after their appearance at auction.

I have also provided estimates on the number of Mint State or Proof coins that have survived for each issue in the Walking Liberty Half Dollar series. These estimates are based on figures listed in the *PCGS Population Report* and *NGC Census*, as well as my own experience handling Walking Liberty Half Dollars that have been consigned to major auctions during the ten-year period from 1999-2008. The population figures provided by PCGS and NGC are useful in determining relative rarity between issues in the Walking Liberty Half Dollar series, but they should not be used to assess absolute rarity. Both the *PCGS Population Report* and *NGC Census* are skewed by resubmissions of the same coin(s) in an effort to obtain a higher grade. Although both services encourage the submitter to return old inserts, these small yet valuable pieces of paper are often discarded before PCGS and NGC have the opportunity to update their population figures.

Likewise, the values that I have provided for each issue in the Walking Liberty Half Dollar series are estimates and should not be taken as a definitive price range in which you should be able to buy an example in a specific grade. Values for Walking Liberty Half Dollars fluctuate yearly, if not monthly and it is important to conduct your own market research in order to determine the current market value of an individual coin. My value estimates are based largely on prices realized data published by leading auction firms as well as select knowledge of private treaty sales.

Each date and mintmark analysis concludes with a section entitled Collecting and Investing Strategies. In this section you will find useful tips and hints, as well as potential pitfalls to avoid concerning the various issues in the Walking Liberty Half Dollar series. The goal of this section is to pass on the considerable knowledge about these coins that I have amassed during the years that I have served as a numismatic professional. It is my hope that the lessons that I have learned and observations that I have made will help you acquire the finest example of each issue in this series that your money can buy. Of course, I also hope that my knowledge and experiences will help you maximize your enjoyment and investment potential when pursuing this popular series.

Bear in mind that I am offering my opinion about how and what to invest in or collect. Like any collectible or investment, there is no crystal ball listing future values for an entire collection or an individual coin. Gather enough numismatic experts in a room today and they will likely each hold different opinions about the current merits, attributes and even the actual value of a particular coin. In the end, the market dictates. With that said, I do make every effort to point out coins that I believe are undervalued or have greater potential to appreciate in value. It goes without saying, however, that ultimately the choice of what to buy and how much to pay is yours alone. Armed with the right information, you will make better choices. Reading this book is certainly the most important step you will make in that direction as far as the Walking Liberty Half Dollar series is concerned.

CHAPTER ONE

Popular Collecting and Investing Strategies for Walking Liberty Half Dollars

Walking Liberty Half Dollars are extremely popular coins that enjoy one of the largest followings among collectors and investors in the numismatic market. There are several reasons for this, one of which is certainly the beauty of the design. This series was introduced during an era that many numismatists consider to be the golden age of United States coin design. Along with other series from the early 20th century such as the Mercury Dime, Peace Dollar, Indian Half Eagle and Saint-Gaudens Double Eagle, the Walking Liberty Half Dollar represents a level of artistic skill from the designer and a depth of symbolism within the design itself that are simply lacking in coins from other periods of U.S. history. There is perhaps no better indication of the beauty and timelessness of the Walking Liberty Half Dollar than the fact that the United States Mint adopted the obverse design for use in the Silver Eagle series introduced in 1986. The only other classic U.S. coin designs so honored through the American Eagle bullion series are the obverse of the Saint-Gaudens Double Eagle and both sides of the Buffalo Nickel. Like the Walking Liberty Half Dollar, both of those designs also have their origins in the golden age of U.S. coin design.

The Walking Liberty Half Dollar is also a popular series because many issues are readily available and, as such, quite affordable in Mint State. The same simply cannot be said for most other U.S. silver series, including the Flowing Hair, Draped Bust, Capped Bust, Seated Liberty and Barber Half Dollars. I can think of few other ways to more easily spark collector and investor interest in a U.S. coin type than the ability to purchase a bright, fully lustrous and minimally abraded example for less than $200. This is all the money you will need to purchase an MS-65 for common-date Walking Liberty Half Dollars such as the 1941, 1942, 1943, 1944 and 1945. By way of comparison, the following prices realized should give you an idea of what you will have to pay to acquire Gem-quality examples of some of the more common issues in the various U.S. Half Dollar series produced from 1794-1915:

- **1795 Flowing Hair Half Dollar NGC MS-65**: realized $92,400 at auction in February of 1995. (This coin would have brought well in excess of $100,000 had it been offered at auction in 2007.)
- **1807 Draped Bust Half Dollar, Large Eagle Reverse NGC MS-65**: realized $29,900 at auction in July of 2004.
- **1826 Capped Bust Half Dollar PCGS MS-65**: realized $8,825 at auction in August of 2007.
- **1875-S Seated Half Dollar, Motto PCGS MS-65**: realized $3,220 at auction in September of 2007.
- **1892 Barber Half Dollar PCGS MS-65**: realized $2,760 at auction in November of 2007.

While many of the rarer, more conditionally challenging issues in the Walking Liberty Half Dollar series might force you down to the MS-63 or MS-64 grade levels, the cost for such examples will often be significantly less than what it will take to acquire, say, a rarer-date Capped Bust Half Dollar in the same grade.

Another reason why the Walking Liberty Half Dollar series is so popular with collectors and investors is because of its versatility. There are many ways to form a meaningful collection or numismatic investment portfolio that includes one or more Walking Liberty Half Dollars. Let's take a closer look at some of the more popular collecting and investing strategies for this series.

Short Type Set

Assembling a short type set is a great way to get started with coin collecting or numismatic investing because it allows you to build a meaningful holding without having to acquire a large number of coins. Short type sets are usually assembled using coins that share one or more characteristics. Examples of some unifying themes for short type sets are denomination, historic era in which the coins were struck and coin designers. The possibilities are essentially limitless, however, and a short type set allows you great freedom in assembling a collection or portfolio using any criteria that you see fit.

Nevertheless, some strategies for assembling short type sets have proven particularly popular in the numismatic market. Some of the more widely adopted strategies that would have to include an example of the Walking Liberty Half Dollar are:

• **United States Half Dollar Types**. This set could be assembled with just 11 coins or with as many as 19 coins depending on how many different types from the Reeded Edge, Seated Liberty and Kennedy series you want to include. The 19-piece set must include one example of each of the following types:

~ *Flowing Hair (1794-1795)*
~ *Draped Bust, Small Eagle Reverse (1796-1797)*
~ *Draped Bust, Large Eagle Reverse (1801-1807)*
~ *Capped Bust, Lettered Edge (1807-1836)*
~ *Reeded Edge, 50 CENTS Reverse (1836-1837)*
~ *Reeded Edge, HALF DOL. Reverse (1838-1839)*
~ *Seated, No Drapery (1839 only)*
~ *Seated, No Motto (1839-1853, 1856-1866)*
~ *Seated, Arrows & Rays (1853 only)*
~ *Seated, Arrows, No Motto (1854-1855)*
~ *Seated, Motto (1866-1873, 1875-1891)*
~ *Seated, Arrows, Motto (1873-1874)*
~ *Barber (1892-1915)*
~ ***Walking Liberty (1916-1947)***
~ *Franklin (1948-1963)*
~ *Kennedy, Silver (1964 only)*
~ *Kennedy, Silver Clad (1965-1970)*
~ *Kennedy, Copper-Nickel Clad, Eagle Reverse (1971-1974, 1977-Date)*
~ *Kennedy, Bicentennial Reverse (1976 only)*

• United States 20ᵗʰ Century Coin Types. This is another versatile set that can be shortened or expanded depending on how many different types you want to represent for series such as the Lincoln Cent, Buffalo Nickel, Standing Liberty Quarter and Kennedy Half Dollar. You also have the option to include or exclude the gold coinage, although my experience has shown that most collectors that assemble 20ᵗʰ century type sets choose to represent only the minor and silver coinage. (Type sets of 20ᵗʰ century United States gold coins are also extremely popular, but they are usually assembled apart from the minor and silver coinage.) The most expansive 20ᵗʰ century type set that I can think of would be comprised of 47 coins and must include one example of each of the following types:

~ *Indian Cent, Bronze (1864-1909)*

~ *Lincoln Cent, Wheat Ears Reverse, V.D.B. (1909 only)*

~ *Lincoln Cent, Wheat Ears Reverse, Bronze (1909-1942, 1944-1958)*

~ *Lincoln Cent, Zinc-Coated Steel (1943 only)*

~ *Lincoln Cent, Memorial Reverse, Bronze (1959-1982)*

~ *Lincoln Cent, Copper-Plated Zinc (1982-Date)*

~ *Liberty Nickel, CENTS Reverse (1883-1912)*

~ *Buffalo Nickel, Type I (1913 only)*

~ *Buffalo Nickel, Type II (1913-1938)*

~ *Jefferson Nickel, Regular Comp., Mintmark Rev. (1938-1942, 1946-1967)*

~ *Jefferson Nickel, Wartime Alloy (1942-1945)*

~ *Jefferson Nickel, Regular Composition, Mintmark Obverse (1968-2003)*

~ *Barber Dime (1892-1916)*

~ *Mercury Dime (1916-1945)*

~ *Roosevelt Dime, Silver (1946-1964)*

~ *Roosevelt Dime, Copper-Nickel Clad (1965-Date)*

~ *Barber Quarter (1892-1916)*

~ *Standing Liberty Quarter, Type I (1916-1917)*

~ *Standing Liberty Quarter, Type II, Pedestal Date (1917-1924)*

~ *Standing Liberty Quarter, Recessed Date (1925-1930)*

~ *Washington Quarter, Silver (1932-1964)*

~ *Washington Quarter, Copper-Nickel Clad, Eagle Rev. (1965-1974, 1977-1998)*

~ *Washington Quarter, Bicentennial Reverse (1976 only)*

~ *Statehood Quarter (1999 and 2000-dated issues only; 10 coins total)*

~ *Barber Half Dollar (1892-1915)*

~ ***Walking Liberty Half Dollar (1916-1947)***

~ *Franklin Half Dollar (1948-1963)*

~ *Kennedy Half Dollar, Silver (1964 only)*

    ~ Kennedy Half Dollar, Silver Clad (1965-1970)
    ~ Kennedy Half Dollar, Copper-Nickel Clad, Eagle Rev. (1971-1974, 1977-Date)
    ~ Kennedy Half Dollar, Bicentennial Reverse (1976 only)
    ~ Morgan Silver Dollar (1878-1921)
    ~ Peace Silver Dollar, High Relief (1921 only)
    ~ Peace Silver Dollar, Low Relief (1922-1935)
    ~ Eisenhower Dollar, Eagle Reverse (1971-1974, 1977-1978)
    ~ Eisenhower Dollar, Bicentennial Reverse (1976 only)
    ~ Susan B. Anthony Dollar (1979-1999)
    ~ Sacagawea Dollar (2000-Date)

• **Classic United States Coin Designs**. This set is a great way to highlight those coin designs that are universally regarded as being among the most beautiful and popular in the history of the United States Mint. Again, this set can be shortened or expanded depending on whether you want to include both minor and silver coinage and/or based on the number of types you want to represent for series such as the Buffalo Nickel, Standing Liberty Quarter and Peace Dollar. The most comprehensive set that you can build using this strategy must include one example of each of the following types:

    ~ Buffalo Nickel, Type I (1913 only)
    ~ Buffalo Nickel, Type II (1913-1938)
    ~ Mercury Dime (1916-1945)
    ~ Standing Liberty Quarter, Type I (1916-1917)
    ~ Standing Liberty Quarter, Type II, Pedestal Date (1917-1924)
    ~ Standing Liberty Quarter, Recessed Date (1925-1930)
    *~ **Walking Liberty Half Dollar (1916-1947)***
    ~ Peace Silver Dollar, High Relief (1921 only)
    ~ Peace Silver Dollar, Low Relief (1922-1935)

• **United States Coin Designs by Adolph A. Weinman**. An often overlooked strategy, this short type set can be completed with the purchase of just two coins:

    ~ Mercury Dime (1916-1945)
    *~ **Walking Liberty Half Dollar (1916-1947)***

Regardless of which short type set you choose to assemble, I recommend that you use an example of one of the most common issues in the Walking Liberty Half Dollar series. I also suggest that you acquire a coin that grades MS-65 or MS-66. Gem-quality Walking Liberty Half Dollars are beautiful coins, and common issues such as the 1941, 1942, 1943, 1944 and 1945 are readily obtainable in these grades. Expect to pay only $100-$200 for an MS-65, while the price will increase to just $200-$400 for an MS-66.

Complete Type Set

A complete type set of United States coins comprises one example of each type of regular-issue, non-commemorative coin struck in the United States Mint. Whether you choose to build your set with minor, silver and gold coins or just minor and silver coins, you are going to have to acquire an example of the Walking Liberty Half Dollar. Regardless of which strategy you choose, or how expansive you choose to make your set, I suggest acquiring a common-date Walking Liberty Half Dollar (the P-mint issues from 1941-1945 are great type candidates) that grades MS-65 or MS-66.

Advanced Type Sets

There are several ways to modify a short or complete type set to increase your level of difficulty, financial requirement and, hopefully, your upside potential when the time comes to sell. Two strategies that will affect how you approach the Walking Liberty Half Dollar series come readily to mind.

Rarer Issues: This strategy requires that you obtain one of the more challenging and, hence, costly issues of each type that you are representing in your set. I have even met a few collectors that are assembling advanced type sets of key-date issues, although I do not recommend that particular strategy unless you have ample resources of time and money.

There are many issues in the Walking Liberty Half Dollar series that would work well for advanced type purposes. For a slightly greater financial commitment above a 1941, 1942, 1943, 1944 or 1945, try an issue like the 1936, 1937 or 1940. An MS-65 will set you back just $200-$300. If your penchant is for earlier dates, the 1917 is the obvious choice. Expect to pay $800-$900 for an MS-65. If a price in that range is too rich for your blood, you could acquire a 1917 in MS-64 for considerably less at $250-$400. If you take your time and cherrypick you should be able to locate an MS-64 that is only marginally less so strong in the categories of technical quality and eye appeal than a coin that grades MS-65.

You could also select a 1933-S to represent the Walking Liberty Half Dollar in an advanced type set. This is perhaps my favorite type candidate in the entire series as examples are highly lustrous and almost always possessed of a razor-sharp, if not full strike. The '33-S costs considerably more than even the 1917, however, and an MS-65 will require you to part with $2,500-$3,500. MS-64s are in the vicinity of $1,250-$2,000, while in MS-63 the price for this issue is in the range of $1,000-$1,200. I do not recommend purchasing a coin that grades MS-62 or below for this requirement. A low-end Mint State example will be either noticeably abraded or lackluster, and these features detract from the strong technical quality and eye appeal that make the 1933-S so appealing for advanced type purposes.

Issuing Mint: Another strategy for expanding a short or basic type set is to include one example from each United States coinage facility in which a given type was struck. For the Walking Liberty Half Dollar series, this increases your requirement to three coins. Focusing on the most common issues, I would select a 1941, 1942, 1943, 1944 or 1945 to represent the Philadelphia Mint. The Denver requirement is also easily met with late-date issues such as the 1942-D and 1947-D. The San Francisco Mint will be a bit more challenging to represent in an advanced type set due to the fact that most S-mint Walking Liberty Half Dollars are poorly struck. You can, however, keep your cost down and have a better-than-average chance of locating a fairly well-struck coin by looking to the 1945-S or 1946-S.

As with most other type sets in which you will have to represent the Walking Liberty Half Dollar, I suggest using coins that grade MS-65 when pursuing this strategy. One example each of the 1941, 1942-D and 1946-S in MS-65 will cost you a total of $350-$800. Such a wide estimate is due to the fact that your purchase price for the 1942-D and

1946-S could vary considerably depending on whether you select an example with an above-average strike or one with virtually full definition.

Proof Type Set

This is an underdeveloped form of type set building, a fact that is largely due to the fact that many U.S. coins are unknown in proof format. Another consideration is the fact that the most common proof issue in many series carries a higher price tag than the most common business strike. On the positive side, however, proof coins are almost always fully struck, and most possess a deeply mirrored finish that can be particularly attractive when viewed on either a brilliant or minimally toned coin. Additionally, proof coins are almost always more carefully produced and preserved than business strikes, which can make it easier to locate a pristine-looking example for inclusion in your type set.

Should you choose to apply this strategy to the completion of a type set of United States coinage, I suggest focusing on the proof 1941 or proof 1942 when you come to the Walking Liberty Half Dollar series. These are the two most plentiful proofs of the type, and they are the most reasonable as far as cost is concerned. Enough high-grade examples have survived for both issues that I would not purchase a coin that grades lower than Proof-65. In that grade, expect to pay $500-$750 for either a proof 1941 or a proof 1942. In Proof-67, you can acquire a representative of either issue for $800-$1,200.

Assembling a Partial Set

Unlike many other series in U.S. numismatics, the Walking Liberty Half Dollar is easily divided into two or three subseries for ease of collecting. The divisions first came about through the efforts of coin album manufacturers that, due to the number of issues, had to split this series between multiple albums. Many collectors and investors that grew up filling coin albums with circulated Walking Liberty Half Dollars have remained faithful to these divisions and chose to assemble partial sets when they moved on to Mint State examples. As such, this is one of the most popular ways to collect this series. Some collectors consider the assembly of a partial set their final goal for the Walking Liberty Half Dollar series, while others assemble a partial set as a stepping stone on the road to building a complete set.

Although the divisions of the Walking Liberty Half Dollar series first came about as a useful expedient for coin album manufacturers, they also serve as excellent parameters for grouping the individual issues according to their relative rarity in Mint State. Opinions differ on whether this series should be divided into two or three portions, but I personally believe that a tripartite division is the most accurate from a numismatic standpoint. Such a division also allows you the greatest flexibility when assembling your collection or investment portfolio. Any of the following three partial sets would serve as an impressive numismatic holding in their own right, or you could choose to build your complete set one partial set at a time.

Early-Date Issues: A partial set of early-date Walking Liberty Half Dollars must include one example of each issue struck from 1916-1933. This is the least popular partial set in the Walking Liberty Half Dollar series. Many collectors that adopt a partial set strategy for this series do so in an effort to keep their overall cost to a minimum. To be successful in their endeavor, these collectors naturally have to exclude the early-date issues from their partial set since the most costly Walking Liberty Half Dollars are largely concentrated in the 1916-1933 date range.

Should you choose to assemble this partial set, I suggest using a mix of coins that grade MS-63, MS-64 and MS-65. I usually do not advise such a strategy since many collectors and investors like to assemble sets of uniform quality. The early portion of the Walking Liberty Half Dollar series, however, is comprised of issues that vary considerably in rarity and cost at the Mint State grade level. Issues such as the 1917, 1929-D and 1929-S are relatively affordable in MS-65, while key-date coins like the 1919-D, 1921-D and 1921-S are costly even in MS-63. As an indication of what it will cost to build a set of early-date Walking Liberty Half Dollars, you are going to need at least $70,000 to acquire just the 1917-S Obverse, 1919, 1919-D, 1919-S, 1921, 1921-D and 1921-S in MS-63.

Middle-Date Issues: This portion of the Walking Liberty Half Dollar series is comprised of those issues dated 1934 through 1940. These issues are much more obtainable in Mint State than those from the early portion of this series, and I recommend assembling this partial set using coins that grade MS-65. There are still some relatively costly issues among the middle-date Walking Liberty Half Dollars, and the 1934-D, 1934-S, 1935-D, 1935-S and 1938-D will set you back anywhere from $1,000-$4,500 each in MS-65. In order to complete this 19-coin partial set in MS-65, you should have at least $17,000 to spend.

Late-Date Issues: This is the easiest partial set of Walking Liberty Half Dollars to assemble, and it is comprised of those issues dated 1941 through the series' end in 1947. This set is often called the Walking Liberty Half Dollar "Short Set," although I have seen some numismatists reserve that term for a set of both the middle-date and late-date issues. Indeed, many collectors choose to combine these two subseries into a single partial set of 1934-1947 Walking Liberty Half Dollars. This is an attractive strategy if you want more of a challenge than the largely common-date 1940s issues will provide but your collecting budget precludes serious pursuit of the more costly early-date issues. Focusing just on the late-date issues, a complete set from 1941-1947 in MS-65 will set you back at least $5,250.

Assembling a Complete Set

Over ten years as a professional numismatist, I have cataloged for auction or otherwise handled several complete sets of Walking Liberty Half Dollars – a testament to the popularity of this strategy among collectors and investors. There are four types of complete sets that you should consider assembling for this series.

Year Set: To successfully complete this set for the Walking Liberty Half Dollar series, you will need to acquire 25 coins. Each example must be from a different year in which the United States Mint struck Half Dollars of this type, and I would focus on the most common issue of the year. I also recommend assembling your year set using coins that grade MS-64. While it is tempting to go for MS-65s or even MS-66s for late-date issues such as the 1941 and 1943, the cost of such examples can be prohibitive for more conditionally challenging issues such as the 1923-S, 1927-S and 1928-S (the only options for their respective years). By building a year set of Walking Liberty Half Dollars that grades MS-64 you will be getting relatively high, uniform technical quality at a fraction of the price that it would cost to assemble a set of MS-65s.

Expect to pay a total at least $30,000 for one Walking Liberty Half Dollar from each of the 25 years in which this series was produced. This cost assumes that you will select coins that grade MS-64 for the most common issues from each year – a strategy that still leaves you with some costly issues such as the 1919, 1921, 1923-S, 1927-S and 1928-S. On the other hand, the same strategy pursued using coins that grade MS-65 will require you to pay at least $70,000.

The issues that I recommend for the year set strategy are:

~ *1916*
~ *1917*
~ *1918*
~ *1919*
~ *1920*
~ *1921*
~ *1923-S (only option)*
~ *1927-S (only option)*
~ *1928-S (only option)*
~ *1929-D*
~ *1933-S (only option)*
~ *1934*
~ *1935*
~ *1936*
~ *1937*
~ *1938*
~ *1939*
~ *1940*
~ *1941*
~ *1942*
~ *1943*
~ *1944*
~ *1945*
~ *1946*
~ *1947*

Date and Mint Set: This strategy dictates that you obtain one example of each business strike issue in the Walking Liberty Half Dollar series. The requirement is for 65 coins – a total that includes examples of both mintmark placements for the 1917-D and 1917-S. This is a very popular collecting and investing strategy for Walking Liberty Half Dollars in the U.S. rare coin market of the 21st century, although it is by no means an inexpensive one if you choose to focus on the Mint State grades. Nevertheless, I insist that you use only Mint State coins to assemble your date and mint set so as to maximize your investment potential in this series. The greatest demand for Walking Liberty Half Dollars in today's market is for Mint State coins, which means that there will be more potential buyers for a Mint State set that one comprised of circulated coins.

I particularly like the prospects of assembling this set using coins that grade either MS-64 or MS-65. Unlike with a year set, I am comfortable with the idea of assembling a date and mint set of this series using a mix of near-Gems and Gems. A date and mint set requires you to contend with all of the series' key-date issues, and I believe that it is perfectly acceptable to include a rare 1921-S that grades MS-64 alongside a common 1943 in MS-65.

A complete 65-coin date and mint set of Walking Liberty Half Dollars comprised solely of coins that grade MS-64 will require you to spend at least $175,000. The same set assembled using MS-65s is considerably more costly at a minimum of $425,000. A set built using a mix of MS-64s and MS-65s will cost between $175,000 and $425,000, the exact price total depending on the exact grade that you select for each issue.

Proof Set: This is an easy task as far as the Walking Liberty Half Dollar series is concerned, as a complete set of proofs is comprised of just seven coins. Strong collector and investor demand keeps costs fairly high, however, particularly for the key-date 1936. Assemble this set with coins that grade at least Proof-65. Even in Proof-67 you will find that all seven issues in this proof series are plentiful enough that the entire set could be assembled within the space of just one year. In Proof-65, your financial burden for this strategy will be at least $8,000. Expect to part with no less than $16,500 for a set of Proof-67s.

Registry Set: These sets are essentially partial or complete sets of one form or another, but they are assembled using the highest-graded coins listed at PCGS and/or NGC. While you could, for example, assemble a PCGS Registry Set of Walking Liberty Half Dollars that grades MS-62, in practice the concept behind these sets is to pit collectors and investors against one another with the goal being to assemble the highest-graded set possible. Both PCGS and NGC maintain Registry Set programs, but whereas PCGS allows only its own coins on the Set Registry, NGC will accept coins certified by both services.

As of January 2008, there are more than 600 Walking Liberty Half Dollar sets registered at PCGS and NGC. These sets are grouped under several different categories, among which are year sets, business strike sets from 1916-1947 and proof sets. I am particularly fond of the Registry Set concept because there is a strong motivating factor in numismatics when you can track your progress and rate your achievement against those of other collectors. This is true even if you are not competing for the top ranking on the PCGS or NGC Registry. For more information on Registry Sets, visit the PCGS and NGC websites at www.pcgs.com and www.ngccoin.com, respectively.

CHAPTER TWO

Considerations for Buying Walking Liberty Half Dollars

As the value of rare United States coins has steadily increased, so too has the number of sellers in the market. Most dealers are honest, reputable experts who thoroughly enjoy buying, selling and studying coins. Many of them even got their start in the industry as collectors, and almost all possess tremendous knowledge of rare coins and the market in which they trade. What's more, reputable dealers are usually very willing to share their expertise and offer sound advice that can prove invaluable when building a meaningful collection or investment portfolio. The benefits of a relationship with a recognized industry expert are numerous, and you should get to know as many reputable dealers as possible and enlist their aid in the attainment of your collecting and/or investing goals. This advice is particularly sound if you are planning on specializing in Walking Liberty Half Dollars. There are some dealers in the market that also specialize in these beautiful coins, and their buying and selling activities often provide them with comprehensive, up-to-date information that may not be available in print.

There are many possible ways to find a reputable United States coin dealer. Chartered by Congress in 1891, the American Numismatic Association (ANA) is the leading hobby organization in U.S. numismatics. The association's website, www.money.org, maintains a searchable database of member dealers. Another excellent source is the Professional Numismatists Guild (PNG), an organization of rare coin and paper money experts whose members are held to high standards of integrity and professionalism. Members of the PNG can be found at the organization's website, www.pngdealers.com. Both the ANA and the PNG are non-profit organizations.

One of the most underutilized methods of finding a reputable numismatic dealer is simply to ask other collectors and investors for recommendations. Word-of-mouth can be a powerful tool. Honest, knowledgeable dealers will enjoy a good reputation among veteran buyers, while less-trustworthy individuals or companies are often treated accordingly in the collector and investor communities. A prerequisite for carrying out this kind of research might be to join a local, regional or national numismatic association. Not only can membership in an organization such as the ANA put you in touch with other collectors and investors, but it could provide access to research tools, current events and other useful technical and market information.

Many of the coins that trade in today's numismatic market pass through auctions instead of being bought and sold outright by dealers. Auction houses are also excellent places to buy Walking Liberty Half Dollars. The catalogs that these firms produce not only strive to provide detailed descriptions of a coin's physical attributes, but they often contain a wealth of historical and analytical information. The best sources for finding reputable auction houses are the ANA, PNG and by word-of-mouth.

Auctioneers offer another powerful, yet underutilized tool for the Walking Liberty Half Dollar specialist: the lot viewing sessions that take place in the weeks or days leading up .o an auction. Through these venues, you can view large numbers of Mint State and proof Walking Liberty Half Dollars, as well as many circulated examples of key-date issues such as the 1919, 1919-D, 1919-S, 1921, 1921-D, 1921-S and, to a lesser extent, the 1938-D. And the more coins that you view, the more familiar you will become with third-party grading standards for this series and issue-specific characteristics such as strike, luster and toning. If schedules and budgets permit, I strongly suggest spending some time at auction lot viewings. Registration is required to participate, but it is almost always free. Furthermore, I have yet to encounter an auctioneer that has made it mandatory to bid after you register. In other words, you should be able to view lots even if you are not interested in bidding in that particular sale.

After finding a reputable dealer and/or auctioneer, what else should you consider before buying your first Walking Liberty Half Dollar? Whether you are a veteran collector or a beginner, it is a good idea to acquire only those pieces that have been graded and encapsulated by Professional Coin Grading Service (PCGS) or Numismatic Guaranty Corporation (NGC). Founded in 1986 and 1987, respectively, these two firms revolutionized the numismatic industry. Coins submitted to these services are evaluated by teams of professional numismatic graders and authenticators. Pieces that are determined to be genuine, unaltered and problem-free for their respective level of preservation are assigned a numeric grade on a 1-70 scale. The coins are then sonically sealed in tamper-evident plastic holders with a paper insert that lists the date, denomination, grade, variety (if applicable) and a unique barcode for identification purposes. Once certified by PCGS or NGC, a coin carries a grade that can help to determine the level at which it will trade in the market. PCGS and NGC-certified coins enjoy universal acceptance, and they also have a high level of liquidity due to the strong reputations that these firms enjoy. In short, PCGS and NGC are the standards for the rare coin industry of the 21st century. They provide a measure of confidence for both novice and veteran collectors when trading in a dynamic market.

It is important to consider that grading is subjective, particularly since both PCGS and NGC take into account a coin's eye appeal when assigning a grade. A characteristic that I consider attractive in a Walking Liberty Half Dollar might be construed as a negative either in your eyes or in the eyes of the expert graders at PCGS and NGC. For example, I might prefer fully brilliant coins with frosty-white surfaces that are free of even the lightest toning. You, however, could be assembling a Walking Liberty Half Dollar set with coins that possess richly original, multicolored toning on both sides. It is always a good idea to evaluate coins – even certified pieces – firsthand before buying. In-person inspection will allow you to get comfortable with a coin's assigned grade and determine whether or not the piece will make an attractive addition to your set.

One other aspect of third-party grading as it pertains to Walking Liberty Half Dollars is critically important in order to be successful at collecting and/or investing in this series. A perusal of the significant examples listings within my analyses of each issue in this series will reveal that there is sometimes considerable variation between the prices that two different Walking Liberty Half Dollars of the same issue trade for even if they have been certified by PCGS and NGC at the same grade level. Striking quality, in particular, can play an integral part in determining the value of a Walking Liberty Half Dollar, especially for issues that are recognized as strike rarities. PCGS and NGC certainly take strike into account when determining their final grade assessment for Walking Liberty Half Dollars. A coin that does not display at least above-average definition by the standards of its respective issue will not grade above a certain level (usually MS-64 or MS-65). On the other hand, there can be considerable difference in cost between a 1942-S in MS-66 with only above-average definition and another example in the same grade with a virtually full strike. Additionally, PCGS and NGC sometimes apply slight different grading standards when evaluating certain issues in this series. Make sure you are familiar with the striking characteristics of the issue, as well as the standards applied by PCGS and NGC, before you buy a high-grade Walking Liberty Half Dollar. This book provides much of the information that you will need in this regard, but it may also be a good idea to enlist the aid of a reputable, trustworthy dealer when the time comes to buy. It would be even better if you had a personal relationship with one or more dealers that specialize in Walking Liberty Half Dollars. Some numismatic professionals might even be willing to evaluate a coin that is being offered through auction and help you determine the optimum level at which to bid.

CHAPTER THREE

A Brief History of the Walking Liberty Half Dollar

The Design

The Walking Liberty Half Dollar was designed by Adolph Alexander Weinman (December 11, 1870 – August 8, 1952). Weinman was born in Karlsruhe, Germany but immigrated to the United States in 1880 at the age of 10. He studied at Cooper Union and the Arts Students League and was a classmate of Augustus Saint-Gaudens, designer of the Indian Eagle and Saint-Gaudens Double Eagle.

Examples of Weinman's architectural sculpting work can be seen on the state capitol buildings in Louisiana, Missouri and Wisconsin, as well as the Jefferson Memorial and the U.S. Supreme Court in Washington, D.C. He is perhaps best remembered, however, for his design of the Mercury Dime and Walking Liberty Half Dollar for the U.S. Mint. This is ironic because Weinman became highly offended when introduced as a numismatist on at least one occasion. Instead, he preferred that people refer to him as an architectural sculptor.

Weinman's design for the Walking Liberty Half Dollar features a full-length representation of Liberty striding to the viewer's left on the obverse. Liberty is wearing a gown, and the American flag is draped around her body. Her left hand holds an olive branch of peace, while her right is outstretch toward a rising sun. The word LIBERTY is inscribed along the upper border, the motto IN GOD WE TRUST is in the lower-right field and the date is in exergue at the lower border. On the reverse, a majestic bald eagle strides toward the viewer's left atop a rocky crag. The eagle is clutching a pine branch in its right talon, above the tip of which is the Latin motto E PLURIBUS UNUM. The legend UNITED STATES OF AMERICA is above and the denomination HALF DOLLAR is below. The mintmark position is in the obverse field below the motto IN GOD WE TRUST for the 1916-D, 1916-S and portions of the 1917-D and 1917-S issues. For all subsequent Denver and San Francisco Mint issues, the mintmark position was changed to the lower-left reverse border.

Throughout its entire production life, the basic design of the Walking Liberty Half Dollar remained unchanged. The Mint did tinker with the finer elements of the design in 1918, 1937 and 1938, introducing new hubs in each of those years. The differences are minor and do not constitute distinct types.

The design of the Walking Liberty Half Dollar is, in my opinion, the most striking and symbolic ever used on a regular-issue, non-commemorative United States coin of this denomination. Weinman executed this design at a time when Europe was being ravaged by the First World War, and the ever-increasing likelihood of American involvement in that conflict was at the forefront of national news throughout 1916. Indeed, his representation of Liberty striding to the East and, in particular, the aggressive stance of the reverse eagle can be interpreted as a warning to the Central Powers that the United States would fight to defend its freedom. This freedom was particularly threatened by Germany's resumption of unrestricted submarine warfare in January of 1917 – a move that contributed to the United States' official declaration of war later that year.

Yearly Mintages & Distribution

Regular-issue production of Walking Liberty Half Dollars commenced in 1916 at the Philadelphia, Denver and San Francisco Mints. These are the only three coinage facilities in which Half Dollars of this type were struck, the Philadelphia Mint also producing proofs for sale to collectors from 1936-1942. Mintages at all three Mints were fairly heavy through 1918 due to an expansion of the United States' economy during the First World War. Production of Walking Liberty Half Dollars fell off markedly in 1919 as the nation returned to a peace-time economy. Limited mintages for the 1919, 1919-D and 1919-S explain the key-date status of these three issues.

The third Philadelphia Mint building contributed all 20 P-mint business strike issues in the Walking Liberty Half Dollar series, as well as the seven proof deliveries. (Image Courtesy of the Historical Society of Philadelphia)

Although Half Dollar production returned to pre-1919 levels in 1920, they fell off even more precipitately in 1921. In fact, only the San Francisco Mint struck more than half a million Half Dollars in 1921, and even the total mintage for the 1921-S is just 548,000 pieces. Much of the blame for the low-mintage, key-date status of the 1921, 1921-D and 1921-S must be attributed to the resumption of Morgan Dollar production that year. Indeed, mintages for Mercury Dimes and Standing Liberty Quarters also suffered in 1921 as all three operating Mints struggled to produce as many Morgan Dollars as possible in fulfillment of the terms of the 1918 Pittman Act.

I also believe, however, that reduced demand for new Half Dollars in economic channels also helps to explain the limited mintages achieved during 1921. Further proof for this theory can be seen in the erratic production of Walking Liberty Half Dollars during the 1920s. No examples were struck in any Mint during 1922, 1924, 1925 or 1926. Additionally, only the San Francisco Mint struck Half Dollars in 1923, 1927 and 1928, probably as a result of a sudden demand for this denomination in the Western states. Half Dollar production in 1929 was limited to the Denver and San Francisco facilities.

No Half Dollars were struck from 1930 through 1932 due to the dire economic situation that prevailed in the United States as a result of the Great Depression. The San Francisco Mint, however, did strike 1.7 million examples in 1933, but the Philadelphia and Denver Mints would not produce any Half Dollars until the following year.

The Denver Mint struck 21 issues in this series.

The Walking Liberty Half Dollars struck from 1916 through 1928 saw extensive commercial use, and relatively few examples were set aside at the time of issue. As such, these issues are much rarer in all Mint State grades than most later-date deliveries in this series. While the 1929-D, 1929-S and 1933-S are also among the scarcer Walking Liberty Half Dollars in Mint State, a decent number of examples were probably kept from entering circulation at the time of striking due to the economic effects of the Great Depression. While some of those coins may have entered circulation beginning in 1934, it seems that many Mint State examples passed directly into numismatic circles from storage in federal vaults. This theory, if true, explains why the 1929-D, 1929-S and 1933-S are somewhat easier to obtain in Mint State than most of the earlier-dated issues in this series.

The San Francisco Mint, here represented by the old mint building that was replaced by a newer facility in 1937, contributed 24 issues to the Walking Liberty Half Dollar series. (Image Courtesy of the San Francisco History Center, San Francisco Public Library)

Beginning in 1934 and continuing through the series' end in 1947, Walking Liberty Half Dollar production was virtually continuous at all three operating Mints. The only exceptions came in 1938 and 1947, when the San Francisco Mint refrained from producing any Half Dollars, and also in 1940, when the Denver Mint did likewise. The 1938-D is the only low-mintage issue among the middle and late-date deliveries in this series, and it commands a premium in all grades even though Mint State examples are not particularly rare in an absolute sense. With the possible exception of the 1937-D, all other Walking Liberty Half Dollars struck from 1934 through 1947 have generous, if not significant original mintages. These issues were saved in greater or lesser quantities in Mint State, and examples at that level of preservation are more-or-less obtainable in today's market, if only in lower grades through MS-64.

CHAPTER FOUR

Date & Mintmark Analysis of Walking Liberty Half Dollars

Courtesy of Bowers and Merena

SPECIFICATIONS

Years Issued: *1916-1947*
Issuing Mints: *Philadelphia, Denver, San Francisco*
Designer: *Adolph Alexander Weinman*
Weight: *12.50 grams*
Composition: *90% Silver, 10% Copper*
Precious Metal Content: *0.36169 ounces of pure silver*
Diameter: *30.6 millimeters*
Edge: *Reeded*

The information in this section is based on my experience handling thousands of Walking Liberty Half Dollars that were cataloged for auction, bought and sold, or otherwise entered the market over the ten-year period from 1999 to 2008.

What follows is the first serious attempt to rank the business strike and proof issues in this series in terms of overall rarity in Mint State/Proof and rarity in high grades (MS-65/Proof-65 or finer). The results are located at the beginning of each date and mintmark analysis, as well as in the appendices at the end of this book. After a brief introductory paragraph entitled General Comments, you will then find my observations concerning Strike, Luster, Surfaces, Toning and Eye Appeal for the issue. I have also provided pricing for significant examples, estimates on the number of Mint State or Proof coins that have survived for each issue and vital pricing estimates. Each date and mintmark analysis concludes with a section entitled Collecting and Investing Strategies.

1916

MINTAGE
608,000

RARITY RANKINGS

Overall, Mint State: 26th of 65
High Grade, MS-65 or Finer: 26th of 65

EARLY-DATE ISSUES
(1916-1933)

Overall, Mint State: 24th of 26
High Grade, MS-65 or Finer: 25th of 26

Important Varieties: None.

General Comments: As the first Philadelphia Mint issue in the Walking Liberty Half Dollar series, the 1916 was saved in significant quantities at the time of striking. The new design was well received among the contemporary public, and many examples were set aside as keepsakes. As a result, Mint State examples are more common in today's market than the limited mintage might suggest. The 1916, however, is somewhat scarce from a market availability standpoint because examples are in such strong demand for first-year type purposes. This is particularly true of coins that grade MS-65 or finer.

Strike: The typical example is sharply struck with good definition over Liberty's head and right (facing) hand on the obverse, as well as the eagle's breast and trailing leg feathers on the reverse. The portion of the flag and the skirt lines that overlay Liberty's forward leg are always softly detailed due to the manner in which the Mint prepared the dies.

Luster: The 1916 is usually satiny in texture, although a few pieces have more of a softly frosted appearance. Many examples have a decided rippled effect to the surface texture; this feature is seen quite often on 1916 and 1917-dated Walking Liberty Half Dollars.

Surfaces: Surface preservation is above average for this issue, with the typical example displaying only a few small, well-scattered abrasions. The 1916 is also a relatively easy Walking Liberty Half Dollar to locate with overall smooth surfaces. Superb Gems that approach perfection, however, are in very short supply.

Toning: Although there are a fair number of brilliant coins from which to choose, the 1916 typically displays at least a bit of light toning on one or both sides. Several examples are quite heavily toned with deep charcoal, antique-copper and/or russet colors that tend to be concentrated in the protected areas around the devices and at the rims.

Eye Appeal: A well-produced and carefully preserved issue, the 1916 has strong eye appeal. In fact, this is one of the most attractive issues in the pre-1934 Walking Liberty Half Dollar series.

Significant Examples:

• **NGC MS-68.** *Ex: Vanek Collection (Heritage, 7/2007), lot 998, where it realized $25,300.*

• **NGC MS-67.** *Ex: ANA Charlotte National Money Show Auction (Heritage, 3/2007), lot 1026, where it realized $7,188; Houston, TX U.S. Coin Signature Auction (Heritage, 11/2007), lot 60986, where it realized $6,900.*

• **NGC MS-67.** *Ex: Long Beach Sale (Heritage, 2/2000), lot 6455, where it realized $6,325.*

Total Known in Mint State: 1,450-1,725 Coins

TOTAL KNOWN BY GRADE			
MS-60 to MS-63	**MS-64**	**MS-65**	**MS-66 or Finer**
575-675 Coins	500-600 Coins	250-300 Coins	120-140 Coins

VALUES BY GRADE			
MS-60	**MS-63**	**MS-65**	**MS-67**
$250-$350	$400-$500	$1,250-$1,600	$7,500-$15,000

COLLECTING AND INVESTING STRATEGIES

With so many attractive coins from which to choose, it is best to avoid any 1916 Walking Liberty Half Dollar with a below-average strike, subdued luster and/or excessively abraded surfaces.

Several Choice and Gem-quality examples are rather darkly toned. Although these coins are original, the market for rare United States coins in the 21st century places great emphasis on bright, "flashy" pieces. In other words, a darkly toned example will probably not perform well when the time comes to sell. Numerous Mint State coins have survived with brilliant surfaces, and others that were once lightly toned have been dipped to bring out the full vibrancy of the mint luster. All other things being equal, these pieces are preferable to a coin with dark and/or splotchy toning.

1916-D

MINTAGE
1,014,400

RARITY RANKINGS

Overall, Mint State: 27th of 65
High Grade, MS-65 or Finer: 24th of 65

EARLY-DATE ISSUES
(1916-1933)

Overall, Mint State: 25th of 26
High Grade, MS-65 or Finer: 24th of 26

Important Varieties: A bold repunched mintmark variety is known with remnants of the first D clearly visible below and slightly to the left of the primary mintmark. The attributions Breen-5130, Fox V-101 and FS-501 all refer to this variety. Examples are very rare in all grades.

General Comments: As a first-year issue, the 1916-D was saved to such an extent that it is now the most common Denver Mint issue in the early Walking Liberty Half Dollar series. The 1916-D is even a bit more plentiful than the 1916 in terms of total number of Mint State examples known. In high grades, however, the 1916-D is rarer than the 1916. Gems are scarce from a market availability standpoint, and Superb Gems are nothing short of rare.

Strike: The 1916-D was generally minted to a high standard of quality, although the strike is not quite as sharp as that seen on the typical 1916. When present, softness of detail is usually confined to Liberty's right (facing) hand on the obverse and the eagle's breast and trailing leg feathers on the reverse. A few pieces are also softly struck over Liberty's head, but almost never to the extent seen on many S-mint issues from 1916-1929.

Luster: Luster is almost always of the satiny type, and it can be a bit subdued even on high-grade examples. The 1916-D is seldom as radiant as the Denver Mint issues from the 1930s and 1940s.

Surfaces: Scattered abrasions are a bit more pronounced for this issue than they are for the 1916. MS-64s with minimally abraded surfaces are still fairly easy to come by, however, and even MS-65s can be had without too much difficulty.

Toning: Even more so than the 1916, the 1916-D is an issue that is characterized by original toning. Deep charcoal, antique-copper and russet colors are sometimes seen. These colors are usually confined to the protected areas at the rims and around the devices. Several examples that I have seen, however, are darkly toned throughout. Such pieces will usually grade no higher than MS-64 if the toning is heavy enough to obscure the luster.

Bright, flashy 1916-D Half Dollars with brilliant surfaces are in relatively short supply in today's market, and such pieces can sometimes command a premium. The example pictured at the beginning of this section was probably dipped at one time – notice the faint remnants of toning still clinging to some of the protected areas at the rims.

Eye Appeal: As an issue, the 1916-D has only average eye appeal. While most examples are well produced, and many are minimally abraded, the luster could be more vibrant. Even more significantly, many examples display dark and/or mottled toning that prevents full appreciation of the design and, thus, limits the eye appeal.

Significant Examples:

• **NGC MS-67.** *Ex: San Francisco Rarities Sale (Bowers and Merena, 7/2005), lot 598, where it realized $10,638.*
• **NGC MS-67.** *Ex: Robert Moreno Collection (Heritage, 7/2005), lot 10002; Dallas, TX Signature Auction (Heritage, 11/2005), lot 2156, where it realized $16,100. The coin did not sell in the first-listed auction.*
• **PCGS MS-67.** *Ex: FUN Signature Sale (Heritage, 1/2004), lot 2090, where it realized $20,700.*

Total Known in Mint State: 1,600-1,850 Coins

TOTAL KNOWN BY GRADE			
MS-60 to MS-63	**MS-64**	**MS-65**	**MS-66 or Finer**
725-825 Coins	550-650 Coins	225-275 Coins	80-100 Coins

VALUES BY GRADE			
MS-60	**MS-63**	**MS-65**	**MS-67**
$275-$375	$450-$550	$1,750-$2,500	$20,000-$30,000

COLLECTING AND INVESTING STRATEGIES

Insist on a sharply struck example with bright, vibrantly lustrous surfaces. I have even handled a few pieces with full striking definition over the highest elements of the design. These are particularly attractive when both sides are brilliant or possessed of only light toning.

1916-S

MINTAGE
508,000

RARITY RANKINGS

Overall, Mint State: *13th of 65*
High Grade, MS-65 or Finer: *19th of 65*

EARLY-DATE ISSUES
(1916-1933)

Overall, Mint State: *13th of 26*
High Grade, MS-65 or Finer: *19th of 26*

Important Varieties: None.

General Comments: Although its mintage is only 100,000 coins fewer than the 1916, the 1916-S is rarer in all Mint State grades, in part because fewer examples of the 1916-S were set aside at the time of issue. Nevertheless, the 1916-S is still one of the easier San Francisco Mint issues in the early Walking Liberty series to locate in high grades.

Strike: This is the most softly struck of the three 1916-dated issues. Most examples have at least a bit of striking incompleteness over the central highpoints. On some pieces, Liberty's head is also affected. On the other hand, the difficulty of locating a well-struck 1916-S Half Dollar has been overstated in the past. The 1916-S is nowhere near as poorly defined as some of the true strike rarities in this series such as the 1918-S, 1942-S and 1944-S. Because the detail over Liberty's left (facing) thigh is also soft due to the manner in which the Mint prepared the dies for this issue, I recommend focusing on Liberty's head and right (facing) hand, as well as the eagle's breast and trailing leg feathers, when evaluating striking quality for the 1916-S.

Luster: The luster is almost always satiny in texture and often slightly subdued.

Surfaces: Most Mint State examples have a few scattered abrasions that rule out a grade higher than MS-63 or MS-64. Considerable patience is required to locate a relatively smooth example in MS-65, to say nothing of a premium-quality Gem or Superb Gem.

Toning: Most Mint State coins have light-to-moderate toning. On the other hand, dark, unsightly toning is not as prevalent for the 1916-S as it is for the 1916 and 1916-D.

Eye Appeal: The 1916-S has slightly above-average eye appeal and, as a whole, the issue is a bit easier to locate with a pleasing appearance than the 1916-D. The strike, although it is seldom full, is actually a bit bolder than most people realize. In addition, dark, splotchy toning is not as plentiful for this issue as it is for the 1916 and 1916-D. When present on a 1916-S, excessively dark toning also tends to be fairly well confined to the peripheries, thereby leaving the centers with a softer, relatively brighter appearance.

Significant Examples:

- **PCGS MS-67.** *Ex: Nicholas Collection (Heritage, 5/2004), lot 7605, where it realized $33,350.*
- **NGC MS-67.** *Ex: Louis E. Eliasberg, Sr. Collection (Bowers and Merena, 4/1997), lot 2139, where it realized $12,100; Lindesmith Collection (Bowers and Merena, 3/2000), lot 654. The coin did not sell in the latter auction.*
- **PCGS MS-66.** *Ex: Pre-Long Beach Sale (Ira & Larry Goldberg, 9/2002), lot 389, where it realized $7,475.*
- **PCGS MS-66.** *Ex: Lindesmith Collection (Bowers and Merena, 3/2000), lot 655, where it realized $6,900.*
- **NGC MS-66.** *Ex: Nicholas Collection (Heritage, 5/2004), lot 7604, where it realized $14,950; Robert Moreno Collection (Heritage, 7/2005), lot 10003, where it realized $12,650; Dallas Signature Auction (Heritage, 12/2005), lot 2120; Atlanta, GA ANA Signature Auction (Heritage, 4/2006), lot 754, where it realized $11,500. The coin did not sell in the December, 2005 sale.*
- **PCGS MS-66.** *Ex: William & Harrison Hiatt Registry Collection of Walking Liberty Half Dollars (Heritage, 1/2005), lot 7543, where it realized $11,500; CSNS Signature Auction (Heritage, 5/2005), lot 7325, where it realized $14,950.*

Total Known in Mint State: 575-700 Coins

TOTAL KNOWN BY GRADE			
MS-60 to MS-63	**MS-64**	**MS-65**	**MS-66 or Finer**
275-325 Coins	175-225 Coins	100-125 Coins	20-25 Coins

VALUES BY GRADE			
MS-60	**MS-63**	**MS-65**	**MS-67**
$1,000-$1,200	$1,500-$2,000	$4,500-$5,250	$27,500-$40,000

COLLECTING AND INVESTING STRATEGIES

There are enough sharply struck 1916-S Half Dollars in the market that you should not have to settle for a poorly defined example or pay a premium just because the coin is touted as having an above-average strike. The 1916-S is just not as difficult to locate with a good strike as many people think. Unlike the 1916 and 1916-D, you could do very well selecting an originally toned 1916-S for your set. Many such pieces are only lightly toned and the more attractive ones have pretty iridescent overtones in gold, apricot, pinkish-silver and/or pearl-gray colors. As with the 1916 and 1916-D, avoid darkly toned examples, particularly if the patina completely envelops the surface on one or both sides.

1917

MINTAGE
12,292,000

RARITY RANKINGS

Overall, Mint State: 34th of 65
High Grade, MS-65 or Finer: 28th of 65

EARLY-DATE ISSUES
(1916-1933)

Overall, Mint State: 26th of 26
High Grade, MS-65 or Finer: 26th of 26

Important Varieties: None.

General Comments: The 1917 has the highest mintage of any Walking Liberty Half Dollar struck prior to 1936, and it is the most common issue in the early portion of this series. Examples are readily obtainable in all grades up to and including MS-65. Premium-quality Gems in MS-66 are surprisingly scarce, however, and there are no more than five Superb Gems known.

Strike: With such a large number of coins produced, it should come as no surprise to read that striking quality varies somewhat for the 1917. The typical example, however, is boldly-to-sharply struck with little, if any softness to the central highpoint detail. Persistence will be rewarded with a fully struck example as such pieces do exist.

Luster: Like the 1916, the 1917 is usually satiny in texture but occasionally encountered with a softly frosted finish. The texture is either smooth or possessed of a slightly rippled appearance.

Surfaces: Examples vary from noticeably abraded to overall smooth, but be warned that the 1917 is more difficult to locate with virtually pristine surfaces than the high mintage might suggest.

Toning: I have seen both brilliant and deeply toned examples, but coins with at least some degree of original patina are more plentiful in the market. Some of the toned coins are highly attractive with vivid colors that can include orange-russet and crimson-red shades.

Eye Appeal: The 1917 has excellent eye appeal, and this is one of the most consistently attractive issues in the early (i.e., pre-1934) Walking Liberty Half Dollar series.

Significant Examples:

• **PCGS MS-67.** *Ex: GBW Collection; Anne Kate Collection (Bowers and Merena, 11/2006), lot 3268, where it realized $24,150.*

Total Known in Mint State: 2,450-2,850 Coins

TOTAL KNOWN BY GRADE			
MS-60 to MS-63	**MS-64**	**MS-65**	**MS-66 or Finer**
1,100-1,300 Coins	900-1,000 Coins	375-425 Coins	90-110 Coins

VALUES BY GRADE			
MS-60	**MS-63**	**MS-65**	**MS-67**
$100-$150	$150-$200	$800-$900	$15,000-$25,000

COLLECTING AND INVESTING STRATEGIES

Do not be afraid to be overly picky when pursuing the 1917. For an early issue in the Walking Liberty Half Dollar series, the 1917 has a generous population in most Mint State grades. Not only is there a sizeable number of coins from which to choose, but the 1917 varies in striking quality and luster type. In addition, the survivors range from fully brilliant to richly toned. Regardless of exactly which grade you choose to represent this issue, make sure you select a coin that meets all of your criteria for technical quality and eye appeal.

Obverse Mintmark
1917-D

MINTAGE
765,400

RARITY
RANKINGS
Overall, Mint State: *18th of 65*
High Grade, MS-65 or Finer: *15th of 65*

EARLY-DATE ISSUES
(1916-1933)
Overall, Mint State: *18th of 26*
High Grade, MS-65 or Finer: *15th of 26*

Important Varieties: None.

General Comments: This Denver Mint issue is the last of only two in the Walking Liberty Half Dollar series that displays the D mintmark in the obverse field below the motto IN GOD WE TRUST. The original mintage is limited for a 20th century United States Half Dollar, and the 1917-D Obverse is one of the rarer Walking Liberty Halves in grades through MS-64. Gems are also elusive, and the 1917-D Obverse is rarer in high grades than the 1916-D, 1916-S, 1928-S, 1929-D, 1929-S and 1933-S. MS-66s are seldom offered, and neither PCGS nor NGC has certified a single coin as a Superb Gem (December/2007).

Strike: This is a generally well-struck issue, although most examples will have a touch of softness to the detail over Liberty's head and right (facing) hand on the obverse. The reverse tends to be a bit better struck but, once again, expect to see a bit of softness in isolated areas such as the eagle's breast and the inside of the trailing leg. Persistence will be rewarded, however, as there are some 1917-D Obverse Half Dollars where incompleteness of strike is barely perceptible.

Luster: The typical example has soft, satiny luster. Most Mint State coins that I have seen are not particularly vibrant in the luster category, and a bright, flashy piece represents an important buying opportunity.

Surfaces: Scattered abrasions are the norm for the issue, and many examples are quite baggy.

Toning: Like the 1917, the 1917-D Obverse ranges from brilliant to deeply toned. Most examples are lightly toned. The coins that are deeply toned tend to have vivid, highly attractive colors.

Eye Appeal: Eye appeal is above average for this issue, this despite somewhat subdued luster and, in lower Mint State grades, noticeably abraded surfaces.

Significant Examples:

    • **PCGS MS-66.** *Ex: FUN Signature Coin Auction (Heritage, 1/2007), lot 1007. The coin did not sell in that auction.*

    • **NGC MS-66.** *Ex: Rarities Sale (Bowers and Merena, 9/2002), lot 328, where it realized $8,740; Charlotte ANA National Money Signature Sale (Heritage, 3/2003), lot 5998, where it realized $10,105.*

    • **PCGS MS-66.** *Ex: Ally Collection (Heritage, 7/2002), lot 8513, where it realized $13,800; FUN Signature Sale (Heritage, 1/2003), lot 7315, where it realized $19,550.*

Total Known in Mint State: 800-925 Coins

TOTAL KNOWN BY GRADE			
MS-60 to MS-63	**MS-64**	**MS-65**	**MS-66 or Finer**
450-500 Coins	275-325 Coins	70-80 Coins	5-7 Coins

VALUES BY GRADE			
MS-60	**MS-63**	**MS-65**	**MS-67**
$500-$600	$1,000-$1,500	$6,500-$7,500	--

COLLECTING AND INVESTING STRATEGIES

The certified population for this issue at PCGS and NGC drops precipitately beginning at the MS-65 level. With this in mind, I really like premium-quality MS-64s. Look for a coin with a minimal number of small, wispy abrasions, relatively vibrant luster and at least bold striking detail. Pay particular attention to Liberty's head and make sure that it is well struck. Both brilliant and toned coins can be attractive, so personal preference should dictate your choice in this regard.

Reverse Mintmark
1917-D

MINTAGE
1,940,000

RARITY RANKINGS

Overall, Mint State: 11th of 65
High Grade, MS-65 or Finer: 4th of 65

EARLY-DATE ISSUES
(1916-1933)

Overall, Mint State: 11th of 26
High Grade, MS-65 or Finer: 4th of 26

Important Varieties: None.

General Comments: This is an underrated issue in all Mint State grades, especially when compared to the 1917-D Obverse. Although the 1917-D Reverse has a much higher mintage than the 1917-D Obverse, fewer examples were set aside at the time of issue. Rare in grades through MS-64, the 1917-D Reverse is very rare as a Gem and all but unobtainable as a Superb Gem. In fact, this is the rarest Walking Liberty Half Dollar in high grades after only the 1918-D, 1919-D and 1921-S.

Strike: Striking detail for this issue is better than most people realize. In fact, the 1917-D Reverse is actually rather well struck for a mintmarked issue from the early portion of this series. True, most examples are softly impressed over Liberty's head on the obverse and the eagle's trailing leg feathers on the reverse. On the other hand, many pieces are at least boldly defined over Liberty's right (facing) hand and the eagle's breast feathers. There are even a fair number of coins where softness of strike is minor enough to have little effect on the eye appeal.

Luster: The 1917-D Reverse usually displays satiny luster that is more vibrant than that seen on the 1916-D, 1916-S and 1917-D Obverse. A few frosty examples are known, but these are in the minority among Mint State survivors.

Surfaces: Lower-grade Mint State coins through MS-62 usually do not possess an excessive number of abrasions, but rather several moderate-size marks. In MS-63 and MS-

64, the abrasions typically remain moderate in size but are fewer in number. This is an extremely challenging issue to locate without at least one or two noticeable bagmarks.

Toning: As with the other early-date issues in this series, the 1917-D Reverse is typically encountered with some degree of toning. Most original examples are actually moderately-to-heavily toned, and I believe that the majority of brilliant coins that are offered in the market used to be lightly toned but were dipped before being certified.

Eye Appeal: This issue has only average eye appeal. The strike is suitably bold, and the luster is quite vibrant on higher-grade examples, but most pieces are marred by noticeable bagmarks. As well, lower-grade coins through MS-63 often have subdued luster that is sometimes due to the depth of toning.

Significant Examples:

• **PCGS MS-66.** *Ex: Cassano Collection; Ally Collection (Heritage, 7/2002), lot 8514, where it realized $26,450.*

• **PCGS MS-66.** *Ex: FUN Signature Sale (Heritage, 1/2000), lot 6884, where it realized $25,300.*

Total Known in Mint State: 450-550 Coins

TOTAL KNOWN BY GRADE			
MS-60 to MS-63	**MS-64**	**MS-65**	**MS-66 or Finer**
200-250 Coins	200-250 Coins	35-45 Coins	7-10 Coins

VALUES BY GRADE			
MS-60	**MS-63**	**MS-65**	**MS-67**
$750-$850	$1,750-$2,250	$13,500-$15,000	$40,000-$50,000

COLLECTING AND INVESTING STRATEGIES

As with the 1917-D Obverse, the 1917-D Reverse represents a good value in MS-64 given the rarity of higher-graded examples. In order to capitalize on this opportunity, however, you should insist on finding a premium-quality coin at the MS-64 grade level. Look for a coin with bold-to-sharp striking detail in all areas, particularly over Liberty's head, as well as vibrant mint luster. I would stay away from coins with dark and/or splotchy toning as such pieces can be difficult to sell.

Obverse Mintmark

1917-S

MINTAGE
952,000

RARITY
RANKINGS

Overall, Mint State: *6th of 65*
High Grade, MS-65 or Finer: *8th of 65*

EARLY-DATE ISSUES
(1916-1933)
Overall, Mint State: *6th of 26*
High Grade, MS-65 or Finer: *8th of 26*

Important Varieties: None.

General Comments: The 1917-S Obverse is virtually identical to the 1917-S Reverse in high-grade rarity, but it is nearly twice as rare in terms of total number of Mint State examples known. This issue is rare even in lower grades through MS-63. Near-Gems are very rare, and there are no more than 60 coins extant that grade MS-65 or finer.

Strike: The strike is generally well executed with bold-to-sharp definition over the central highpoints, Liberty's head on the obverse and the eagle's trailing leg feathers on the reverse. Some softness of detail is usually present in one or more of these areas, particularly the eagle's trailing leg feathers, but very few examples can be described as poorly struck.

Luster: The 1917-S Obverse almost always has satin luster, and it is usually a bit subdued even on high-grade coins. Luster quality for this issue is very similar to that of the 1916-D, 1916-S and 1917-D Obverse.

Surfaces: To acquire a Mint State 1917-S Reverse Half Dollar you are probably going to have to accept a fair number of small and moderate-size abrasions. This is one of the most challenging issues in this series to locate even with relatively smooth surfaces.

Toning: Deeply toned examples tend to be unattractive with dark and/or splotchy colors. While most of the 1917-S Reverse Half Dollars that I have seen are only moderately or lightly toned, the color on these pieces also tends to inhibit the eye appeal. Many lightly toned examples appear to have been dipped even though the original toning was too deep for the solution to completely remove. What are left on such pieces are usually hazy, dull and/or mottled overtones. Very, very few examples are either completely brilliant or attractively toned.

Eye Appeal: Eye appeal is below average for this issue, an assessment that is due primarily to the difficulty of locating an example that is free of distracting abrasions. Toning also plays a part, as most examples that I have seen are just not attractive in this regard. This is one of the most challenging Walking Liberty Half Dollars to locate with good eye appeal.

Significant Examples:

> • **PCGS MS-66.** *Ex: Ally Collection (Heritage, 7/2002), lot 8515, where it realized $27,600.*

Total Known in Mint State: 300-425 Coins

TOTAL KNOWN BY GRADE			
MS-60 to MS-63	**MS-64**	**MS-65**	**MS-66 or Finer**
135-185 Coins	120-170 Coins	45-55 Coins	4-5 Coins

VALUES BY GRADE			
MS-60	**MS-63**	**MS-65**	**MS-67**
$1,800-$2,300	$4,000-$5,000	$15,000-$20,000	$50,000-$75,000

COLLECTING AND INVESTING STRATEGIES

This is one issue that will almost certainly require you to compromise on eye appeal and, instead, focus exclusively on finding a certified example that fits into your budget. In fact, you will probably have very little control over any characteristics of this issue except for the strike and, to a lesser extent, the toning. Look for a coin with overall bold definition and no areas of excessive lack of detail. Also, try to avoid pieces with unsightly toning, especially if it is dark, hazy and/or splotchy. This is a tall order to fill, but I have seen a (very) few pieces with either brilliant surfaces or relatively attractive toning. As far as luster and abrasions are concerned, just try to find a coin whose surfaces are not completely lackluster or possessed of large, singularly conspicuous bagmarks.

Reverse Mintmark
1917-S

MINTAGE
5,554,000

RARITY RANKINGS

Overall, Mint State: *15th of 65*
High Grade, MS-65 or Finer: *7th of 65*

EARLY-DATE ISSUES
(1916-1933)

Overall, Mint State: *15th of 26*
High Grade, MS-65 or Finer: *7th of 26*

Important Varieties: None.

General Comments: With a sizeable original mintage, you might assume that the 1917-S Reverse is a plentiful coin in Mint State. This is not the case, however. Most examples seem to have slipped quietly into circulation at the time of striking. Coins that grade MS-60 to MS-63 are occasionally available, but they are still rare when viewed in the wider context of this series. MS-64s are very rare, and there are no more than 60 examples that grade MS-65 or finer in numismatic circles. The 1917-S Reverse is rarer in high grades than the 1918-S, as well as the lower-mintage 1919-S, 1920-S, 1923-S, 1927-S and 1928-S.

Strike: The overall strike for the 1917-S Reverse is relatively sharp by the standards of the San Francisco Mint. Nevertheless, virtually all examples that I have seen are softly struck over Liberty's right (facing) hand on the obverse and the eagle's trailing leg feathers on the reverse. A smaller number of coins possess incompleteness of strike at Liberty's head and over the lowermost feathers on the eagle's breast. I have seen fewer than 10 coins that I would classify as being fully struck in all areas.

Luster: Luster is usually satiny, although there are a few examples with more of a softly frosted texture. This issue tends to be a bit more vibrant in the luster category than the 1916-D, 1916-S, 1917-D Obverse and 1917-S Obverse.

Surfaces: The typical 1917-S Reverse has a few wispy abrasions. There are not that many examples with sizeable distractions, but even fewer have an overall smooth appearance.

Toning: There are a few more brilliant examples of the 1917-S Reverse in the market than there are for other early issues in this series such as the 1916-D, 1917-D Obverse and 1917-S Obverse. Still, most examples that I have seen are at least lightly toned, and many are quite extensively patinated. The toning that this issue displays is usually more attractive than that seen for the 1917-S Obverse, and this even applies to coins with deeply toned surfaces.

Eye Appeal: The 1917-S Reverse has above-average eye appeal, and high-grade coins with brilliant or lightly toned surfaces are very attractive.

Significant Examples:

• **PCGS MS-66.** *Ex: Nicholas Collection (Heritage, 5/2004), lot 7618, where it realized $26,450.*

Total Known in Mint State: 675-775 Coins

TOTAL KNOWN BY GRADE			
MS-60 to MS-63	**MS-64**	**MS-65**	**MS-66 or Finer**
400-450 Coins	225-275 Coins	40-50 Coins	8-10 Coins

VALUES BY GRADE			
MS-60	**MS-63**	**MS-65**	**MS-67**
$250-$350	$1,500-$2,000	$10,000-$15,000	$20,000-$30,000

COLLECTING AND INVESTING STRATEGIES

If the 1917-S Obverse is an issue that you will have to compromise on, the 1917-S Reverse is one with which you can afford to be somewhat selective. Yes, this is a scarce-to-rare issue in all Mint State grades, but examples trade frequently enough that even in MS-65 multiple pieces are offered during most years.

Avoid coins with bothersome lack of detail over Liberty's head and the eagle's breast, as well as those on which Liberty's (right) facing hand and/or the eagle's trailing leg feathers are excessively soft in detail. Although lightly toned examples of the 1917-S Reverse can be very attractive, I suggest acquiring a fully brilliant example. Such pieces are obtainable with patience, and they will fit better into a Walking Liberty Half Dollar set where most of the middle and late-date examples are apt to be bright and untoned.

1918

MINTAGE
6,634,000

RARITY
RANKINGS
Overall, Mint State: 17th of 65
High Grade, MS-65 or Finer: 20th of 65

EARLY-DATE ISSUES
(1916-1933)
Overall, Mint State: 17th of 26
High Grade, MS-65 or Finer: 20th of 26

Important Varieties: None.

General Comments: Although widely regarded as a common coin, the 1918 is surprisingly scarce in Mint State for a Philadelphia Mint issue with such a large number of examples struck. This is still, of course, one of the more readily obtainable issues in the early Walking Liberty Half Dollar series in grades through MS-65. There are fewer than 15 MS-66s listed at the two leading certification services, however, and no Superb Gems (December/2007). The 1918 is grossly underrated in all Mint State grades when compared to the 1916 and 1916-D, both of which have much lower mintages but were saved in greater numbers due to their first-year status. In high grades, the 1918 is also rarer than the 1917, 1929-D, 1929-S and 1933-S.

Strike: The 1918 usually comes with a sharp strike, and the issue is rarely offered with less than bold definition. I have even seen a decent number of examples where the strike is virtually full. Softness of detail, when present, is usually minor and most readily evident in the center of the obverse over and around Liberty's right (facing) hand.

Luster: The 1918 has excellent luster that is either of a satin or frosty type. Both luster types are quite vibrant on examples of this issue, particularly in the finer Mint State grades.

Surfaces: The typical Mint State 1918 Half Dollar is lightly abraded and grades MS-63 or MS-64. Large, overly conspicuous bagmarks are hardly ever seen on examples of this issue.

Toning: This issue seldom displays dark toning. When present, in fact, toning is usually a pale, iridescent or bright, vivid color. There are also many fully or nearly brilliant examples from which to choose.

Eye Appeal: The 1918 has strong eye appeal that is a reflection of the care with which the issue was produced and the fact that most Mint State examples are bright, highly lustrous and minimally abraded.

Significant Examples:

• **PCGS MS-67.** *Ex: Anne Kate Collection (Bowers and Merena, 11/2006), lot 3285; Baltimore Auction (Bowers and Merena, 3/2007), lot 4370, where it realized $9,488. The coin did not sell in the first-listed auction.*

• **NGC MS-66.** *Ex: Palm Beach, FL Signature Sale (Heritage, 3/2005), lot 5845; San Francisco, CA ANA Signature Auction (Heritage, 7/2005), lot 6407. The coin did not sell in either auction appearance.*

• **PCGS MS-66.** *Ex: CSNS Signature Sale (Heritage, 5/2003), lot 6869, where it realized $5,980; Robert Moreno Collection (Heritage, 7/2005), lot 10009, where it realized $11,500.*

• **NGC MS-66.** *Ex: FUN Signature Sale (Heritage, 1/2005), lot 7579. The coin did not sell in that auction.*

Total Known in Mint State: 700-850 Coins

TOTAL KNOWN BY GRADE			
MS-60 to MS-63	**MS-64**	**MS-65**	**MS-66 or Finer**
300-350 Coins	275-300 Coins	125-175 Coins	10-12 Coins

VALUES BY GRADE			
MS-60	**MS-63**	**MS-65**	**MS-67**
$450-$550	$800-$900	$2,500-$4,000	--

COLLECTING AND INVESTING STRATEGIES

If you are looking for a better-date type coin from the early Walking Liberty Half Dollar series, look no further than the 1918. This issue is almost always well struck with vibrant luster. Even in MS-63 or MS-64 you should be able to locate an example that is free of overly distracting abrasions. Both lightly toned and brilliant coins are usually very attractive.

1918-D

MINTAGE
3,853,040

RARITY RANKINGS

Overall, Mint State: 14th of 65
High Grade, MS-65 or Finer: 3rd of 65

EARLY-DATE ISSUES (1916-1933)

Overall, Mint State: 14th of 26
High Grade, MS-65 or Finer: 3rd of 26

Important Varieties: None.

General Comments: In an absolute sense, the 1918-D is rarer than such other early mintmarked issues in this series as the 1917-D Obverse, 1917-S Reverse, 1918-S and 1927-S. In high grades, the 1918-D has an even more impressive rating – it is the third-rarest issue in the entire Walking Liberty Half Dollar series. Deficiencies with the strike and/or scattered abrasions prevent most examples from grading higher than MS-64. PCGS and NGC have seen a few exceptional coins, all of which have been certified as MS-66 (December/2007).

Strike: The typical 1918-D is softly struck on the obverse at Liberty's right (facing) hand and on the reverse over the eagle's breast and trailing leg feathers. Liberty's head can also be affected by inadequate striking pressure, but it is usually bold-to-sharp in appearance even when other areas of the coin are lacking in detail.

Luster: Satin luster is the norm for this issue, although I have seen the occasional frosty example pass through auction or show up in a dealer's inventory.

Surfaces: It is very difficult to locate a 1918-D whose surfaces are free of even a few light, wispy abrasions.

Toning: The 1918-D is usually encountered with light or moderate toning. There are not all that many brilliant examples in the market and most of these have probably been dipped. Toning for this issue tends to be indifferent. In other words, it is seldom either particularly beautiful or noticeably displeasing.

Eye Appeal: Overall eye appeal for this issue is slightly below average. Striking quality and abrasions are usually an impediment to locating an attractive, high-grade example, while neither the luster nor the toning is particularly impressive. MS-66s, however, are usually very attractive, and the same could also be said for a few high-end MS-65s.

Significant Examples:

• **NGC MS-66.** *Ex: Robert Moreno Collection (Heritage, 7/2005), lot 10010; Dallas, TX Signature Auction (Heritage, 11/2005), lot 2162, where it realized $25,300. The coin did not sell in the first-listed auction.*

Total Known in Mint State: 625-725 Coins

TOTAL KNOWN BY GRADE			
MS-60 to MS-63	**MS-64**	**MS-65**	**MS-66 or Finer**
280-330 Coins	300-350 Coins	30-40 Coins	4-5 Coins

VALUES BY GRADE			
MS-60	**MS-63**	**MS-65**	**MS-67**
$1,000-$1,250	$2,250-$2,750	$18,000-$23,000	--

COLLECTING AND INVESTING STRATEGIES

With such a significant increase in cost from the MS-64 to the MS-65 grade level, I suggest acquiring a premium-quality MS-64 for your set. Try to locate a 1918-D with at least emerging definition over the central highpoints and, if possible, frosty mint luster. If you must buy a toned coin, which will probably be the case, acquire an example with lighter, preferably iridescent overtones that do not inhibit the luster.

1918-S

MINTAGE
10,282,000

RARITY RANKINGS

Overall, Mint State: 19th of 65
High Grade, MS-65 or Finer: 9th of 65

**EARLY-DATE ISSUES
(1916-1933)**

Overall, Mint State: 19th of 26
High Grade, MS-65 or Finer: 9th of 26

Important Varieties: None.

General Comments: The 1918-S has the highest mintage of any San Francisco Mint Walking Liberty Half Dollar struck before 1942. The United States' economy was in full swing during the final year of World War One and, with a pressing need for new coinage in the avenues of commerce, the majority of coins entered circulation. With so few saved at the time of issue, the 1918-S is a scarce-to-rare coin even in lower Mint State grades. In fact, the 1918-S is similar in overall rarity to the lower-mintage 1917-D Obverse. The 1918-S is extremely difficult to locate in MS-65 and virtually unobtainable any finer. The 1918-S is rarer in high grades than the key-date 1919-S, as well as the 1920-S, 1923-S and 1927-S.

Strike: Fully struck 1918-S Walking Liberty Half Dollars simply do not exist. Virtually all Mint State coins will have some degree of striking incompleteness over the central highpoints. The coin pictured above, for example, is noticeably flat in the center of the obverse. Many are also poorly defined at Liberty's head and the eagle's trailing leg feathers. I have even seen a few examples with surfaces that were smooth and lustrous enough to grade MS-65 but were placed into MS-64 holders at PCGS and NGC because Liberty's head was completely flat. The third-party grading services seem to require at least a modicum of detail to Liberty's head before assigning an MS-65 grade to an early-date Walker.

Striking quality varies considerably among the 1918-S survivors. There are actually quite a few examples in the market with a bold-to-sharp strike. Additionally, even many poorly struck coins that I have seen possess at least emerging definition over Liberty's right (facing) hand. This is most evident as separation between the thumb and the index finger.

Luster: The 1918-S comes with both satin and frosty luster, but the former is a bit more plentiful among survivors. There are some really vibrant examples that grade MS-64 or finer and, as a whole, the 1918-S has good luster.

Surfaces: Surface preservation is above average for this issue. As previously stated, deficiencies with the strike have prevented some otherwise Gem-quality coins from obtaining an MS-65 grade. This means that some MS-64s that you will encounter in the market are going to have smoother surfaces than you would normally expect for the grade.

Toning: Examples come in all appearances from brilliant to deeply toned. The typical 1918-S is lightly-to-moderately toned, and these coins tend to be quite attractive.

Eye Appeal: Although this might surprise some readers, I believe that the 1918-S has slightly above-average eye appeal. Luster is quite good, and excessively abraded surfaces are seldom a problem. What's more, there are more boldly struck coins than most people realize. As long as you do not insist on 100% full striking detail, it should really not be all that difficult to locate a relatively pleasing example.

Significant Examples: PCGS and NGC list five 1918-S Half Dollars at the MS-66 and MS-67 grade levels (December/2007). Unfortunately, I have been unable to locate an auction appearance for one of those coins.

Total Known in Mint State: 825-950 Coins

TOTAL KNOWN BY GRADE			
MS-60 to MS-63	**MS-64**	**MS-65**	**MS-66 or Finer**
400-450 Coins	375-425 Coins	50-60 Coins	4-5 Coins

VALUES BY GRADE			
MS-60	**MS-63**	**MS-65**	**MS-67**
$400-$500	$1,500-$2,000	$12,500-$17,500	$50,000-$75,000

COLLECTING AND INVESTING STRATEGIES

The difficulty of locating a 1918-S with relatively bold striking detail is overstated in many numismatic references and auction catalogs. A perusal of sales and dealer inventories suggests there are quite a few decently struck examples in the market. Most have at least emerging detail over the central highpoints, and Liberty's head can be quite bold. However, do not insist on acquiring a fully struck example as you will probably never make a purchase! Just try to find a coin with overall bold definition. Patience may even be rewarded with a relatively sharp example.

I would strongly consider acquiring the nicest MS-64 that you can find. Many certified MS-65s are no better struck than an MS-64, and unless you are assembling a Registry Set, a well-struck MS-64 with a few wispy abrasions is preferable to a softly struck MS-65. This is particularly true if you consider that an MS-64 will usually cost no more than $5,000, while an MS-65 will require you to pay at least three times more. If you do stretch for the Gem, make sure you are getting your money's worth by insisting on a strike that is well above-average in all areas.

1919

MINTAGE
962,000

RARITY RANKINGS

Overall, Mint State: 9th of 65
High Grade, MS-65 or Finer: 17th of 65

EARLY-DATE ISSUES
(1916-1933)

Overall, Mint State: 9th of 26
High Grade, MS-65 or Finer: 17th of 26

Important Varieties: None.

General Comments: The 1919 is the rarest Walking Liberty Half Dollar struck in the Philadelphia Mint after only the 1921. Despite a lower mintage, however, it is not as rare as either the 1919-D or 1919-S because more examples were saved. Still, the typical 1919 grades only MS-63 or MS-64, and the certified populations at PCGS and NGC begin to drop off rapidly in MS-65. Gems are rare in an absolute sense, but the 1919 is actually easier to obtain at or above the MS-65 level than many higher-mintage issues from the 1910s and 1920s, such as the 1918-D, 1918-S, 1920-S and 1923-S.

Strike: The 1919 generally has above-average striking detail for an early-date issue in this series. Most examples have suitably bold definition, but even these will have a touch of softness to the detail over the central highpoints and, less often, at Liberty's head. I have seen many examples that are essentially fully struck and essentially fully struck with no significant lack of detail. A smaller number of coins are flatly struck in the centers.

Luster: Frosty coins are the norm. This issue almost always displays excellent luster.

Surfaces: Most 1919 Half Dollars have a few scattered abrasions; these are usually small-to-moderate in size. Even an MS-65 is apt to display one or two stray bagmarks. This issue is very challenging to locate with smooth, virtually pristine surfaces.

Toning: Many examples that I have seen are fully brilliant with bright, radiant surfaces. This is one of the flashier issues in the early Walking Liberty Half Dollar series. When toning is present, it is usually light in color with an iridescent quality and seldom more than moderate in depth.

Eye Appeal: The 1919 has strong eye appeal. The strike is usually bold, if not sharp, and high-grade coins tend to be bright and flashy. As well, even lower-grade Mint State coins seldom have an excessive number of abrasions.

Significant Examples:

• **PCGS MS-67.** *Ex: Ally Collection (Heritage, 7/2002), lot 8520, where it realized $10,350.*

• **PCGS MS-67.** *Ex: FUN Signature Sale (Heritage, 1/1999), lot 6812. The coin did not sell in that auction.*

Total Known in Mint State: 375-525 Coins

TOTAL KNOWN BY GRADE			
MS-60 to MS-63	**MS-64**	**MS-65**	**MS-66 or Finer**
150-200 Coins	135-185 Coins	60-85 Coins	25-50 Coins

VALUES BY GRADE			
MS-60	**MS-63**	**MS-65**	**MS-67**
$1,000-$1,250	$3,000-$3,500	$5,500-$6,500	$15,000-$20,000

COLLECTING AND INVESTING STRATEGIES

This is a well-produced issue, and there is no reason why you should have to settle for an unattractive example at any Mint State grade level. If your numismatic budget will support such an acquisition, I suggest buying a 1919 Walking Liberty Half Dollar that grades MS-65. Such coins are well preserved with a minimum number of trivial abrasions and full, usually frosty luster. What's more, they are in very short supply in the market and are likely to perform much better in the future than lower-grade examples with greater populations. If you insist on purchasing a brilliant or minimally toned Gem, you will also have a bright, flashy coin with eye appeal that it commensurate with its technical quality.

1919-D

MINTAGE
1,165,000

**RARITY
RANKINGS**

Overall, Mint State: 3rd of 65
High Grade, MS-65 or Finer: 1st of 65

**EARLY-DATE ISSUES
(1916-1933)**
Overall, Mint State: 3rd of 26
High Grade, MS-65 or Finer: 1st of 26

Important Varieties: None.

General Comments: A leading strike and condition rarity in the Walking Liberty Half Dollar series, the 1919-D is an important find even in Extremely Fine and About Uncirculated grades. In terms of total number of Mint State coins known, the 1919-D is the third-rarest Walking Liberty Half Dollar after the 1919-S and 1921-S. When we consider only those coins that grade MS-65 or finer, however, the 1919-D emerges as the rarest issue in this series. This issue is all but unobtainable above the MS-65 grade level.

Strike: The typical example is flatly struck in the centers with no definition to Liberty's right (facing) hand on the obverse or the eagle's central breast feathers and trailing leg feathers on the reverse. I have even seen a few coins that are so lightly struck in the centers that a few planchet rollermarks are still discernible in those areas. Additionally, Liberty's head is almost always softly defined. A coin that has even emerging definition in the centers is an important find. I have never seen a 1919-D Half Dollar with 100% full striking detail.

Luster: Luster quality is well below average for this issue. Most examples have a satiny finish that is decidedly muted in appearance.

Surfaces: Although the issue is extremely rare in the finer Mint State grades, the 1919-D seldom possesses a significant number of distracting abrasions. Instead, inferior luster and/or poor striking detail prevent most Mint State survivors from grading finer than MS-64.

Toning: The 1919-D is usually offered brilliant. A fair number of examples are lightly toned, but I have encountered very few pieces with moderate-to-heavy toning.

Eye Appeal: This is one of the most challenging issues in the Walking Liberty Half Dollar series to locate with above-average eye appeal. Poor striking detail bears much of the blame for this assessment, but lackluster surfaces also play a part.

Significant Examples:

- **PCGS MS-66.** *Ex: Palm Beach, FL Signature Sale (Heritage, 11/2004), lot 6903, where it realized $270,250.*
- **PCGS MS-65.** *Ex: Anne Kate Collection (Bowers and Merena, 11/2006), lot 3302, where it realized $172,500.*
- **PCGS MS-65.** *Ex: Jack Lee Collection; Pre-FUN Elite Coin Auction (Superior, 1/2004), lot 718, where it realized $140,875; Robert Moreno Collection (Heritage, 7/2005), lot 10013; Dallas, TX Signature Auction (Heritage, 11/2005), lot 2166, where it realized $103,500. The coin did not sell in the July, 2005 auction.*
- **PCGS MS-65.** *Ex: Gene Holland Collection of United States Coins (Heritage, 1/2005), lot 30238, where it realized $112,125.*
- **PCGS MS-65.** *Ex: William & Harrison Hiatt Registry Collection of Walking Liberty Half Dollars (Heritage, 1/2005), lot 30239, where it realized $97,750.*
- **PCGS MS-65.** *Ex: Elite Coin Auction (Superior, 1/2003), lot 814, where it realized $103,500.*

Total Known in Mint State: 250-375 Coins

TOTAL KNOWN BY GRADE			
MS-60 to MS-63	**MS-64**	**MS-65**	**MS-66 or Finer**
150-200 Coins	100-150 Coins	10-15 Coins	1 Coin

VALUES BY GRADE			
MS-60	**MS-63**	**MS-65**	**MS-67**
$5,000-$6,000	$15,000-$20,000	$100,000-$120,000	--

COLLECTING AND INVESTING STRATEGIES

When you consider that there is a nearly four-fold price increase for the 1919-D between the MS-64 and MS-65 grade levels, a premium-quality MS-64 is a sensible buy. In order to guarantee that the coin you are purchasing really is premium quality for both the issue and the grade, insist on an above-average strike that includes emerging definition to the central highpoints. I have seen the occasional piece with sharp detail over Liberty's hand and the eagle's breast. If you can find one, such a coin would be a great buy.

Expect to pay a premium for a well-struck 1919-D Half Dollar in MS-64. A flatly struck example will probably sell for $25,000-$30,000. On the other hand, I have seen some relatively bold pieces command $40,000+ at auction.

1919-S

MINTAGE
1,552,000

RARITY RANKINGS

Overall, Mint State: 2nd of 65
High Grade, MS-65 or Finer: 10th of 65

EARLY-DATE ISSUES (1916-1933)

Overall, Mint State: 2nd of 26
High Grade, MS-65 or Finer: 10th of 26

Important Varieties: None.

General Comments: In terms of total number of Mint State coins known, the 1919-S is the second-rarest Walking Liberty Half Dollar after the 1921-S. This is a lower-mintage, heavily circulated issue, and even coins that grade MS-60 to MS-64 are rare. Gems are even rarer in an absolute sense, but the 1919-S is not as difficult to locate in high grades as the 1917-D Reverse, 1917-S Obverse, 1917-S Reverse, 1918-S, 1920-D and 1921-D, to say nothing of the 1918-D, 1919-D and 1921-S. A lone MS-67 at NGC is the finest example known to the two leading certification services (December/2007).

Strike: As a whole, the 1919-S has a better strike than the 1919-D. Even most poorly struck 1919-S Half Dollars that I have seen possess a hint of separation between Liberty's thumb and index finger on the right (facing) hand. The same cannot be said for a flatly struck 1919-D. Still, the typical 1919-S is softly defined over the central highpoints on both sides, the eagle's trailing leg feathers and Liberty's head on the obverse.

Luster: The 1919-S has better luster than the 1919-D, although it is not among the most vibrant in this series. Most examples possess either a satiny or softly frosted texture.

Surfaces: This issue seldom has problems with large, individually conspicuous abrasions. Most lower-end Mint State coins are limited in grade by small, wispy abrasions and/or impaired luster.

Toning: Like the 1919-D, the 1919-S is seldom encountered with deeply toned surfaces. The typical example is either brilliant or lightly toned.

Eye Appeal: The 1919-S has stronger eye appeal than the 1919-D, but it is still little better than average when viewed in the wider context of the Walking Liberty Half Dollar series.

Significant Examples:

- **NGC MS-67.** *Ex: Robert Moreno Collection (Heritage, 7/2005), lot 10014; Dallas, TX Signature Auction (Heritage, 11/2005), lot 2168, where it realized $32,200; Dallas, TX Coin Signature Coin Auction (Heritage, 7/2006), lot 2498, where it realized $43,125. The coin did not sell in the first-listed auction.*
- **PCGS MS-66.** *Ex: Ally Collection (Heritage, 7/2002), lot 8522, where it realized $12,650.*
- **NGC MS-66.** *Ex: Rarities Sale (Bowers and Merena, 8/2004), lot 694, where it realized $18,400.*
- **NGC MS-66.** *Ex: ANA National Money Show Auction (Superior, 3/2000), lot 435, where it realized $11,213.*

Total Known in Mint State: 225-350 Coins

TOTAL KNOWN BY GRADE			
MS-60 to MS-63	**MS-64**	**MS-65**	**MS-66 or Finer**
100-150 Coins	75-100 Coins	45-55 Coins	15-20 Coins

VALUES BY GRADE			
MS-60	**MS-63**	**MS-65**	**MS-67**
$2,500-$3,000	$7,500-$9,000	$15,000-$20,000	$45,000-$55,000

COLLECTING AND INVESTING STRATEGIES

I really like the 1919-S in MS-65. Such coins are decidedly rare in an absolute sense, but enough exist that you should be able to acquire an attractive piece after a year or so of diligent searching. In fact, enough MS-65s cross the auction block during a typical 12-month period that you can even afford to be somewhat selective in your purchase. Do not feel as though you have to compromise as much on strike with the 1919-S as you might have to do with the 1919-D. An overall boldly struck MS-65 should not be too difficult to acquire. I also suggest obtaining a coin that has above-average luster quality for the issue. Avoid the few deeply toned Gems that are offered now and then as these tend to be splotchy or otherwise unattractive.

1920

MINTAGE
6,372,000

RARITY RANKINGS

Overall, Mint State: *21st of 65*
High Grade, MS-65 or Finer: *18th of 65*

EARLY-DATE ISSUES
(1916-1933)

Overall, Mint State: *21st of 26*
High Grade, MS-65 or Finer: *18th of 26*

Important Varieties: None.

General Comments: The 1920 is one of the easier early-date Walking Liberty Half Dollars to locate in Mint State, but it is still rarer than the 1916, 1916-D, 1917, 1929-D and 1933-S. Gems are rare when viewed in the wider context of this series, and the 1920 is unknown any finer than MS-66.

Strike: A fairly well-struck issue, most examples will have some definition over the central obverse highpoint even though the strike will not be 100% full in that area. The reverse is usually overall sharp, and Liberty's head is sufficiently bold (if not sharp) on most examples that I have seen.

Luster: The 1920 has good luster that is usually of the frosty type. Dipped pieces are less vibrant with more of a satiny texture.

Surfaces: The typical example will have more noticeable abrasions than most Mint State 1919, 1919-D and 1919-S Half Dollars. Even in lower grades, however, the 1920 seldom has more than one or two sizeable distractions. On the other hand, and of particular detriment to the eye appeal, large bagmarks tend to be concentrated in prime focal areas in and around the centers.

Toning: As a more plentiful and, hence, less costly issue in the finer Mint State grades, the 1920 is not subject to dipping to the same degree as the 1919. As such, there are more moderately toned 1920 Half Dollars in the market. I have even seen many deeply toned examples that hark back to the appearance of many 1916 and 1917-dated Half Dollars. Of course, lightly toned and brilliant coins are also available. Darkly toned 1920 Half Dollars tend to have a more-or-less mottled appearance. On the other hand, the colors are usually relatively vivid and seldom include the subdued russet and/or charcoal shades seen on so many examples of the 1916 and 1916-D.

Eye Appeal: This issue has above-average eye appeal. Even lower-grade Mint State coins through MS-62 are relatively attractive, while Choice and Gem-quality examples are usually very appealing regardless of whether they are brilliant or toned.

Significant Examples:

- **PCGS MS-66.** *Ex: Denver ANA Auction (Bowers and Merena, 8/2006), lot 3434, where it realized $8,338.*
- **PCGS MS-66.** *Ex: Anne Kate Collection (Bowers and Merena, 11/2006), lot 3307, where it realized $18,975.*
- **NGC MS-66.** *Ex: John Jay Pittman Collection (David Akers, 5/1998), lot 1643, where it realized $8,800; Long Beach Signature Sale (Heritage, 2/2002), lot 7035; Pittsburgh, PA Signature Sale (Heritage, 8/2004), lot 6492, where it realized $8,338; CSNS Signature Auction (Heritage, 5/2005), lot 7368, where it realized $5,463. The coin did not sell in the February, 2002 sale.*
- **PCGS MS-66.** *Ex: William & Harrison Hiatt Registry Collection of Walking Liberty Half Dollars (Heritage, 1/2005), lot 7614, where it realized $10,350.*
- **PCGS MS-66.** *Ex: Ally Collection (Heritage, 7/2002), lot 8523, where it realized $9,775.*

Total Known in Mint State: 925-1,050 Coins

TOTAL KNOWN BY GRADE			
MS-60 to MS-63	MS-64	MS-65	MS-66 or Finer
425-475 Coins	400-450 Coins	90-110 Coins	12-15 Coins

VALUES BY GRADE			
MS-60	MS-63	MS-65	MS-67
$250-$300	$550-$650	$4,000-$5,000	--

COLLECTING AND INVESTING STRATEGIES

The 1920 is a great early-date type candidate in the Walking Liberty Half Dollar series. MS-65s are not too prohibitive in cost. They are plentiful enough that you should have several coins from which to choose throughout any given year of numismatic trading. This is nice as it gives you the opportunity to select either a brilliant example or a toned piece depending on your personal taste. Since there are enough original coins in both categories out there, I would avoid a dipped example as the solution can sometimes mute the luster.

1920-D

MINTAGE
1,551,000

RARITY RANKINGS

Overall, Mint State: 5th of 65
High Grade, MS-65 or Finer: 6th of 65

EARLY-DATE ISSUES (1916-1933)

Overall, Mint State: 5th of 26
High Grade, MS-65 or Finer: 6th of 26

Important Varieties: None.

General Comments: The true rarity of the 1920-D is not widely appreciated by those who do not specialize in the Walking Liberty Half Dollar series. In terms of total number of Mint State coins known, the 1920-D is rarer than the 1919 and 1921 – both of which are lower-mintage, key-date issues that are highly regarded in numismatic circles. The typical 1920-D grades only MS-63 or MS-64. This is due to slightly subdued luster and not, as frequently stated by other numismatic writers and catalogers, because of an excessively soft strike. That the 1920-D is one of the easier pre-1934 Walking Liberty Half Dollars from the Denver Mint to locate in high grades underscores the fact that it is not a major strike rarity. Gems, however, are very rare when viewed in the wider context of the numismatic market. The 1920-D is unknown in any grade above the MS-66 level.

Strike: Strike varies widely for this issue, much more so than other mintmarked Half Dollars from this era such as the 1918-D and 1919-S. I have seen examples with both excessively soft striking detail as well as razor-sharp definition. The typical example is actually quite bold, although the central highpoints are apt to be a tad soft, as is Liberty's head. All-in-all, the 1920-D is a fairly well-struck issue.

Luster: Luster quality also varies for this issue. Some examples have pleasing luster with a softly frosted texture. Other pieces are subdued in luster with more of a satiny finish.

Surfaces: Most Mint State examples are only lightly abraded with a few wispy, small-size bagmarks. Large, singularly distracting abrasions are seldom a problem for the 1920-D.

Toning: Given that light toning is the norm for this issue, you may have difficulty locating a fully brilliant example. Even dipped pieces are apt to display remnants of original toning or light, golden-colored secondary toning. Darkly toned pieces, however, are in the minority among Mint State survivors.

Eye Appeal: The 1920-D has better-than-average eye appeal – a conclusion that might come as a shock if you are used to classifying this issue as a major strike rarity. The overall detail on most coins that I have seen is really not that bad. Patience will be rewarded with a piece that also has good luster and pleasing toning.

Significant Examples:

- **NGC MS-66.** *Ex: FUN Signature Sale (Heritage, 1/2005), lot 7621, where it realized $17,825; Robert Moreno Collection (Heritage, 7/2005), lot 10017, where it realized $13,800.*
- **PCGS MS-66.** *Ex: William & Harrison Hiatt Registry Collection of Walking Liberty Half Dollars (Heritage, 1/2005), lot 30244, where it realized $32,200.*
- **PCGS MS-66.** *Ex: Ally Collection (Heritage, 7/2002), lot 8524, where it realized $18,400.*
- **PCGS MS-66.** *Ex: James Bennett Pryor Collection of United States Half Dollars (Bowers and Merena, 1/1996), lot 347, where it realized $12,100.*

Total Known in Mint State: 300-400 Coins

TOTAL KNOWN BY GRADE			
MS-60 to MS-63	**MS-64**	**MS-65**	**MS-66 or Finer**
100-150 Coins	150-200 Coins	40-50 Coins	5-7 Coins

VALUES BY GRADE			
MS-60	**MS-63**	**MS-65**	**MS-67**
$1,250-$1,500	$3,000-$4,000	$10,000-$15,000	--

COLLECTING AND INVESTING STRATEGIES

Catalogers often heap lavish praise upon well-struck examples of the 1920-D that are offered at auction. I have even seen some numismatists compare the 1920-D to the 1919-D in terms of both high-grade and strike rarity. But the 1920-D is not as rare as the 1919-D in the finer Mint State grades and the worst-struck 1920-D Half Dollars are nowhere near as softly defined as the typical 1919-D. In fact, the 1920-D might be the most overrated issue in the entire series.

This is not to imply that the 1920-D is an easy coin to locate with full striking detail. Such pieces are so rare as to be virtually unobtainable. It is just that the typical 1920-D is actually quite bold with acceptable definition to the central highpoints. Thus, I would not use strike as a criteria for deciding whether a particular coin is right for your collection. Instead, focus on other characteristics such as luster, toning and an absence of sizeable or individually distracting abrasions. If you find a Mint State example that meets this criteria, chances are actually quite good that the coin will also possess at least sufficiently bold striking detail.

1920-S

MINTAGE
4,624,000

RARITY RANKINGS

Overall, Mint State: 10th of 65
High Grade, MS-65 or Finer: 14th of 65

EARLY-DATE ISSUES (1916-1933)

Overall, Mint State: 10th of 26
High Grade, MS-65 or Finer: 14th of 26

Important Varieties: None.

General Comments: With a higher mintage, it should come as no surprise to read that the 1920-S is not as rare as the 1920-D in Mint State. This is true for all grades from MS-60 through MS-66. Additionally, the 1920-S is actually obtainable (although still excessively rare) as a Superb Gem whereas the 1920-D is unknown any finer than MS-66. When viewed in the wider context of the Walking Liberty Half Dollar series, however, the 1920-S is a rare coin in grades through MS-63 and very rare any finer. High-grade examples are rarer than those of the 1917-D Obverse and 1928-S, as well as the lower-mintage 1919.

Strike: The 1920-S is very similar to the 1920-D in terms of overall striking quality, although the Denver Mint issue is usually touted as being more of a strike rarity. If anything, the 1920-S is more of a strike rarity than the 1920-D, if only by a very small margin. The typical 1920-S is softly struck over the central highpoints on both sides, as well as the eagle's trailing leg feathers on the reverse and Liberty's head on the obverse. While there are a fair number of coins with emerging definition in the centers, the 1920-S is seldom offered with a bold-to-sharp strike.

Luster: Luster is a strong suit for this issue, and most Mint State examples have vibrant surfaces in either a satiny or softly frosted texture.

Surfaces: Abrasions are seldom a serious stumbling block to locating a pleasing 1920-S Half Dollar in any grades. Moderate-size bagmarks tend to be few in number, while more extensively abraded coins usually have only wispy, small-size distractions.

Toning: There are a few more brilliant examples of the 1920-S on the market than there are for the 1920-D. Still, the typically encountered survivor of this San Francisco Mint issue is lightly toned, often only at the rims. A heavily toned 1920-S Half Dollar is a rarity, and such pieces are usually confined to the lower Mint State grades because the toning is so deep that it has impaired the luster.

Eye Appeal: While the 1920-S has good luster and is seldom encountered with excessively abraded surfaces, the issue is not quite as strong in the eye appeal category as the 1920-D. The reason for this discrepancy is that the 1920-S possesses a slightly poorer quality of strike.

Significant Examples:

- **NGC MS-67.** *Ex: Central States Sale (Heritage, 4/2000), lot 7461. The coin did not sell in that auction.*
- **NGC MS-66.** *Ex: Long Beach Signature Sale (Heritage, 2/2005), lot 7978, where it realized $19,550.*
- **PCGS MS-66.** *Ex: Nicholas Collection (Heritage, 5/2004), lot 7637, where it realized $28,750.*
- **NGC MS-66.** *Ex: Philadelphia 2000 Signature Sale (Heritage, 8/2000), lot 6049, where it realized $8,050.*

Total Known in Mint State: 400-500 Coins

TOTAL KNOWN BY GRADE			
MS-60 to MS-63	**MS-64**	**MS-65**	**MS-66 or Finer**
175-225 Coins	150-200 Coins	60-70 Coins	10-15 Coins

VALUES BY GRADE			
MS-60	**MS-63**	**MS-65**	**MS-67**
$650-$750	$2,500-$3,000	$9,500-$11,500	$20,000-$30,000

COLLECTING AND INVESTING STRATEGIES

Unlike for the 1920-D, the difficulty of locating even a boldly struck 1920-S has been somewhat understated in the past. Any Mint State 1920-S that has more than just emerging definition in the centers and over Liberty's head represents an important buying opportunity. You should seriously consider acquiring such a coin as long as the other technical and aesthetic qualities are equally as strong.

1921

MINTAGE
246,000

RARITY RANKINGS

Overall, Mint State: 7th of 65
High Grade, MS-65 or Finer: 11th of 65

EARLY-DATE ISSUES
(1916-1933)

Overall, Mint State: 7th of 26
High Grade, MS-65 or Finer: 11th of 26

Important Varieties: None.

General Comments: The 1921 has the second-lowest mintage in the entire business strike Walking Liberty Half Dollar series. There is no doubt that this is one of the rarest Walking Liberty Half Dollars in terms of total number of coins known, both circulated and Mint State. When we consider only Mint State grades, however, the 1921 is actually a somewhat overrated issue that is not as rare as the 1917-S Obverse, 1919-D, 1919-S, 1920-D, 1921-D or 1921-S. Nor is the 1921 among the ten-rarest Walking Liberty Half Dollars in high grades, although Gems are still rare in an absolute sense and more challenging to locate than those of such other issues in this series as the 1917-D Obverse, 1920-S, 1923-S and 1927-S.

Strike: The 1921 is a well-struck issue. Most examples are sharply impressed even over the central highpoints. I have seen relatively few coins with bothersome lack of detail, and it is almost always confined to Liberty's head and right (facing) hand on the obverse. Even a softly struck 1921 will usually possess sufficiently bold definition on the reverse, lack of detail to the eagle's breast and trailing leg feathers being less pronounced than a soft strike on the obverse.

Luster: This issue has very good, if not excellent luster that is usually of a frosty type.

Surfaces: The 1921 seldom comes with baggy surfaces. I have even seen several examples in MS-63 and MS-64 where somewhat subdued luster, as opposed to distracting abrasions, precludes a higher grade.

Toning: Most Mint State 1921 Half Dollars are either fully brilliant or only lightly toned. A small percentage of survivors are extensively toned, however, and these coins tend to display rich antique-copper and/or russet colors. Such toning on a 1921 Half Dollar is seldom deep enough to completely obscure the luster, although the mint finish may be slightly muted by its presence.

Eye Appeal: Eye appeal is very strong for the 1921. This issue is well struck with good luster and no real problems as far as abrasions are concerned.

Significant Examples:

• **PCGS MS-66.** *Ex: ANA Sale of the Millennium (Bowers and Merena, 8/2000), lot 4264, where it realized $12,650; Ally Collection (Heritage, 7/2002), lot 8526, where it realized $18,400.*

• **NGC MS-66.** *Ex: Lindesmith Collection (Bowers and Merena, 3/2000), lot 664, where it realized $16,100.*

Total Known in Mint State: 325-450 Coins

TOTAL KNOWN BY GRADE			
MS-60 to MS-63	**MS-64**	**MS-65**	**MS-66 or Finer**
135-185 Coins	130-180 Coins	60-70 Coins	4-6 Coins

VALUES BY GRADE			
MS-60	**MS-63**	**MS-65**	**MS-67**
$3,250-$3,750	$6,250-$7,250	$14,000-$16,000	--

COLLECTING AND INVESTING STRATEGIES

Less rare than the 1921-D and 1921-S, the 1921 is a strong candidate for inclusion in a year set of Walking Liberty Half Dollars. The 1921 would also serve well in an investment portfolio that includes various types of United States coins. With a limited mintage, the issue enjoys strong demand even in the lowest Mint State grades. This is also a well-produced and (for those coins that survived) well-preserved issue. The typical Mint State coin is almost always going to be more attractive than a similarly graded example of the mintmarked issues from 1918-1921. MS-64s and MS-65s are usually very pretty coins regardless of whether they are brilliant or toned. Avoid any 1921 Half Dollar with noticeable bluntness of detail over Liberty's head and right (facing) hand.

1921-D

MINTAGE
208,000

RARITY RANKINGS

Overall, Mint State: 4th of 65
High Grade, MS-65 or Finer: 5th of 65

EARLY-DATE ISSUES
(1916-1933)

Overall, Mint State: 4th of 26
High Grade, MS-65 or Finer: 5th of 26

Important Varieties: None.

General Comments: The lowest mintage in the business strike Walking Liberty Half Dollar series belongs to the 1921-D. Perhaps understandably, this is a rare issue in all Mint State grades. The 1921-D is not quite as rare as the 1919-D, 1919-S or 1921-S in terms of total number of Mint State coins known. On the other hand, this issue is rarer than the 1919-S in high grades. A 1921-D that grades even MS-62 or MS-63 represents an extremely important buying opportunity in any numismatic market. MS-66s are encountered only once in a long while, and there are no Superb Gems graded at either PCGS or NGC (December/2007).

Strike: The 1921-D is only marginally less well-struck than the 1921. Most examples are overall bold with at least some separation between Liberty's right (facing) hand, the stem of the olive branch and the adjacent portion of the American flag. In fact, I have seen quite a few sharply struck coins, but only a relatively small number of examples where Liberty's head and right (facing) hand are noticeably blunt.

Luster: Luster is generally good for this issue, but the 1921-D is seldom as vibrant as the 1921 because it usually displays a satiny rather than frosty texture. The occasional softly frosted 1921-D is encountered, however, and these have excellent luster.

Surfaces: Mint State 1921-D Walking Liberty Half Dollars seldom have an excessive number of abrasions, and those that are present are often small in size. In fact, deficient luster bears almost as much blame as scattered abrasions for confining some examples to lower Mint State grades through MS-63.

Toning: The 1921-D usually displays either brilliant surfaces or has light toning in silver, gold and/or tan shades. Many lightly toned pieces have been dipped to remove deeper patina.

Eye Appeal: Eye appeal is above average for this issue, and the few high-grade coins that have survived are very pretty.

Significant Examples:

- **NGC MS-66.** *Ex: CSNS Signature Auction (Heritage, 5/2005), lot 7380, where it realized $24,725; Dallas, TX Signature Auction (Heritage, 11/2005), lot 2173, where it realized $23,000; Baltimore Auction (Bowers and Merena, 11/2006), lot 3316; FUN Signature Coin Auction (Heritage, 1/2007), lot 1014. The coin did not sell in the last two auctions listed.*
- **PCGS MS-66.** *Ex: Long Beach Signature Auction (Heritage, 2/2006), lot 1421, where it realized $48,875; San Francisco, CA ANA Signature Auction (Heritage, 7/2005), lot 10228; JFS Collection (Heritage, 1/2005), lot 30252, where it realized $48,875; JFS Collection (Heritage, 8/2004), lot 4141, where it realized $39,100; New York, NY Signature Sale (Heritage, 7/2002), lot 8527, where it realized $40,250. The coin did not sell in the July, 2005 auction.*

Total Known in Mint State: 275-375 Coins

TOTAL KNOWN BY GRADE			
MS-60 to MS-63	**MS-64**	**MS-65**	**MS-66 or Finer**
110-160 Coins	115-165 Coins	40-50 Coins	5-6 Coins

VALUES BY GRADE			
MS-60	**MS-63**	**MS-65**	**MS-67**
$3,750-$4,250	$11,500-$13,500	$20,000-$30,000	--

COLLECTING AND INVESTING STRATEGIES

As a low-mintage, key-date issue that enjoys strong numismatic demand, the 1921-D would make an important addition to a collection or investment portfolio in any Mint State grade. Nevertheless, I would acquire a coin that grades MS-63 or finer so as to avoid examples with lackluster surfaces and/or overly distracting abrasions. Whether you purchase a brilliant or lightly toned coin depends on your personal preference, but I would absolutely insist on acquiring a sharply struck example. A sizeable enough percentage of Mint State 1921-D Half Dollars are sharply struck, and acquiring an example with even marginally less detail might impair your ability to obtain top dollar when the time comes to sell.

1921-S

MINTAGE
548,000

**RARITY
RANKINGS**

Overall, Mint State: 1st of 65
High Grade, MS-65 or Finer: 2nd of 65

**EARLY-DATE ISSUES
(1916-1933)**
Overall, Mint State: 1st of 26
High Grade, MS-65 or Finer: 2nd of 26

Important Varieties: None.

General Comments: Although the 1916-S, 1921, 1921-D and 1938-D all have lower mintages, the 1921-S is the rarest Walking Liberty Half Dollar in Mint State. I believe that this issue somehow escaped the attention of contemporary dealers and collectors and was not saved in significant numbers at the time of striking. After the 1919-D, the 1921-S is the second-rarest Half Dollar of this type in high grades. Coins that grade MS-65 or finer are exceedingly rare, MS-66s are virtually unobtainable and Superb Gems are unknown.

Strike: The typical example is softly struck over Liberty's head and right (facing) hand on the obverse. In fact, it is virtually impossible to locate a coin with more than the barest trace of separation between the thumb and index finger. The reverse tends to be better struck, although the eagle's trailing leg feathers are indistinct on many examples that I have seen.

Luster: Satin luster is the norm for this issue, and it is often a bit subdued and not particularly vibrant. Much of this is due to the prevalence of dipped coins in the market, the solution often muting the original mint finish somewhat in addition to removing toning. Overall luster quality, therefore, is below average.

Surfaces: As with the 1921 and 1921-D, the 1921-S almost never displays heavily abraded surfaces. Bagmarks, when present, are usually small in size and/or few in number.

Toning: The 1921-S usually comes brilliant or with minimal toning, and many pieces have been dipped. When a toned example is offered, the surfaces are usually light in color.

Eye Appeal: The 1921-S has the lowest eye appeal rating among the three 1921-dated issues in the Walking Liberty Half Dollar series. Striking quality is poorer than that of the 1921 and 1921-D (although it is far from the worst in this series) and the luster is almost always muted in sheen.

Significant Examples:

- **NGC MS-66.** *Ex: November Signature Sale (Heritage, 11/2003), lot 6877, where it realized $87,400.*
- **PCGS MS-65.** *Ex: Anne Kate Collection (Bowers and Merena, 11/2006), lot 3319, where it realized $161,000.*
- **NGC MS-65.** *Ex: William & Harrison Hiatt Registry Collection (Heritage, 2/2005), lot 7991, where it realized $63,250; Baltimore Auction (Bowers and Merena, 3/2006), lot 1463. The coin did not sell in the latter auction.*
- **PCGS MS-65.** *Ex: December Baltimore Auction (Bowers and Merena, 12/2004), lot 2164, where it realized $77,625; San Francisco Rarities Sale (Bowers and Merena, 7/2005), lot 613, where it realized $92,000.*
- **PCGS MS-65.** *Ex: Nicholas Collection (Heritage, 5/2004), lot 7646, where it realized $109,250.*
- **PCGS MS-65.** *Ex: James Bennett Pryor Collection of United States Half Dollars (Bowers and Merena, 1/996), lot 351, where it realized $44,000.*

Total Known in Mint State: 150-210 Coins

TOTAL KNOWN BY GRADE			
MS-60 to MS-63	**MS-64**	**MS-65**	**MS-66 or Finer**
55-65 Coins	75-100 Coins	25-35 Coins	1-2 Coins

VALUES BY GRADE			
MS-60	**MS-63**	**MS-65**	**MS-67**
$10,000-$15,000	$25,000-$35,000	$75,000-$100,000	--

COLLECTING AND INVESTING STRATEGIES

I do not advise being too picky when it comes to the 1921-S. There are very few Mint State coins from which to choose, and your best chances for securing one will be to select an example that grades MS-63 or MS-64. These are the levels at which most PCGS and NGC-certified examples are concentrated, and they offer considerable value for this issue when compared to a coin that grades MS-65. Even most Gems that I have seen have the soft strike and somewhat muted luster for which this issue is known. A Choice Mint State example with suitable luster quality and at least some separation between the thumb and index finger will not look all that different from an MS-65 as long as there are no sizeable and/or individually distracting abrasions. Unless you are assembling a top-ranked Registry Set, therefore, I suggest picking a premium-quality MS-63 or MS-64 and applying the $25,000-$50,000 that you will save by not buying an MS-65 toward other numismatic purchases. Remember, the 1921-S is the rarest Walking Liberty Half Dollar in Mint State, and Choice examples have tremendous appeal in virtually any numismatic market.

1923-S

MINTAGE
2,178,000

RARITY RANKINGS

Overall, Mint State: 8th of 65
High Grade, MS-65 or Finer: 12th of 65

**EARLY-DATE ISSUES
(1916-1933)**

Overall, Mint State: 8th of 26
High Grade, MS-65 or Finer: 12th of 26

Important Varieties: None.

General Comments: The 1923-S is the only Half Dollar produced by the Mint from 1922 through 1926. This resulted in strong demand in commercial channels and, today, the 1923-S is rarer in all Mint State grades than its sizeable mintage suggests. In fact, the 1923-S trails only the lower-mintage 1917-S Obverse, 1919-S and 1921-S as the rarest San Francisco Mint Walking Liberty Half Dollar. The 1923-S is not ranked as high when we consider only MS-65 or finer grades; both the 1917-S Reverse and 1918-S are rarer in high grades. Still, a Gem 1923-S is a rare coin – rarer even than a Gem 1916, 1916-S, 1917-D Obverse and 1919.

Strike: The typical 1923-S will have only slightly better striking detail than the 1921-S, with a bit more separation between the finer elements of Liberty's right (facing) hand and in the center of the obverse. Additionally, the strike over Liberty's head tends to be better for the 1923-S than the 1921-S. Still, expect to see some striking incompleteness to the central obverse highpoint. Liberty's head can also be affected by inadequate striking detail. The reverse of the typical 1923-S Half Dollar is better struck than the obverse. The eagle's trailing leg feathers are usually indistinct, although the breast feathers are quite sharp on all but a small percentage of coins.

Luster: Most examples are actually quite vibrant. Satiny texture is the norm, but a softly frosted coin is occasionally available.

Surfaces: As a whole, the 1923-S is a more heavily abraded issue than the 1920-S, 1921, 1921-D or 1921-S. Fortunately, bagmarks tend to be small and singularly inconspicuous.

Toning: It is very difficult to locate a 1923-S without some degree of toning or mottled color, and heavily toned examples also turn up once in a while.

Eye Appeal: The 1923-S has above-average eye appeal. While the toning that many examples possess can diminish the overall eye appeal, this feature is almost always offset by vibrant luster and a strike that is above-average by San Francisco Mint standards.

Significant Examples:

- **PCGS MS-66.** *Ex: Anne Kate Collection (Bowers and Merena, 11/2006), lot 3322, where it realized $48,875.*
- **PCGS MS-66.** *Ex: Denver ANA Auction (Bowers and Merena, 8/2006), lot 3448, where it realized $26,450.*
- **PCGS MS-66.** *Ex: Dallas Signature Sale (Heritage, 12/2004), lot 6167; Long Beach Signature Sale (Heritage, 2/2005), lot 7999; CSNS Signature Auction (Heritage, 5/2005), lot 7386, where it realized $14,950; Dallas Signature Auction (Heritage, 12/2005), lot 2148; Long Beach Signature Auction (Heritage, 2/2006), lot 1429, where it realized $31,050.*
- **PCGS MS-66.** *Ex: Nicholas Collection (Heritage, 5/2004), lot 7650, where it realized $34,500.*
- **PCGS MS-66.** *Ex: Ally Collection (Heritage, 7/2002), lot 8529, where it realized $23,000. This coin possesses a nearly full strike, and it is one of the best-produced examples of the 1923-S Half Dollar that I have ever seen.*
- **PCGS MS-66.** *Ex: Lindesmith Collection (Bowers and Merena, 3/2000), lot 665, where it realized $14,950.*

Total Known in Mint State: 375-500 Coins

TOTAL KNOWN BY GRADE			
MS-60 to MS-63	**MS-64**	**MS-65**	**MS-66 or Finer**
160-210 Coins	150-200 Coins	55-65 Coins	15-18 Coins

VALUES BY GRADE			
MS-60	**MS-63**	**MS-65**	**MS-67**
$1,100-$1,300	$3,000-$3,500	$12,000-$15,000	$50,000-$75,000

COLLECTING AND INVESTING STRATEGIES

While you can accept some lack of detail over Liberty's right (facing) hand and the eagle's trailing leg feathers, do not consider purchasing any coin with blunt detail to Liberty's head or the eagle's breast. The latter areas are actually quite well defined on all but a small number of 1923-S Half Dollars.

Toning is a greater stumbling block than strike. Here, look for more evenly toned examples. The prospect of acquiring a coin with unsightly mottled toning is not a pleasant one. I would purchase any fully brilliant 1923-S that has solid technical merits for the grade without even the slightest hesitation.

1927-S

MINTAGE
2,392,000

RARITY RANKINGS

Overall, Mint State: 16th of 65
High Grade, MS-65 or Finer: 13th of 65

EARLY-DATE ISSUES
(1916-1933)

Overall, Mint State: 16th of 26
High Grade, MS-65 or Finer: 13th of 26

Important Varieties: None.

General Comments: Like the 1923-S and 1928-S, the 1927-S is an issue that saw extensive circulation. It is not, however, as rare as either of these issues in terms of total number of Mint State coins known. On the other hand, the 1927-S is virtually identical to the 1923-S in high-grade rarity, and both issues are rarer than the 1928-S at or above the MS-65 level. The 1927-S is also rarer than the lower-mintage 1916, 1916-S, 1917-D Obverse and 1919. The finest examples listed at PCGS and NGC grade MS-66, and these are very rare with a combined population of no more than eight coins at both certification services (December/2007).

Strike: This is one of the most poorly struck issues in the entire Walking Liberty Half Dollar series. The area where Liberty's right (facing) hand is supposed to be is seldom more than just a smooth piece of metal, and the eagle's trailing leg feathers are less well defined than normal for many early mintmarked issues in this series. In addition, more than half of the Mint State coins that I have seen are also softly struck over Liberty's head and the highpoints of the eagle's breast.

Luster: Luster for the 1927-S is far superior to that of the 1921-S, and it is even better than that seen on the typical 1923-S. Unlike these other two issues, the 1927-S usually has a frosty texture to the mint finish.

Surfaces: This is the earliest issue in the Walking Liberty Half Dollar series for which abrasions play a significant role in confining many examples to lower Mint State grades.

Even an MS-64 is apt to display several scattered bagmarks, and one or two of these are often sizeable enough to warrant individual attention.

Toning: Bright, brilliant surfaces or light, even toning are the norm for the 1927-S. Many coins that do possess deeper toning only display this feature at or near the rims.

Eye Appeal: The 1927-S has only average eye appeal. Vibrant, frosty luster and a lack of dark toning for most examples are definite strong suits. On the other hand, soft striking detail and scattered abrasions often limit the grade as well as the eye appeal for many Mint State coins.

Significant Examples:

• **PCGS MS-66.** *Ex: Beverly Hills Rarities Sale (Bowers and Merena, 2/2006), lot 325, where it realized $35,650.*

• **PCGS MS-66.** *Ex: Denver ANA Auction (Bowers and Merena, 8/2006), lot 3449, where it realized $20,700.*

• **NGC MS-66★.** *Ex: John H. Dabbert Collection (Heritage, 7/2003), lot 7830, where it realized $17,250; Robert Moreno Collection (Heritage, 7/2005), lot 10023, where it realized $20,700.*

• **PCGS MS-66.** *Ex: Jack Lee; Pre-FUN Elite Coin Auction (Superior, 1/2004), lot 436, where it realized $24,150.*

Total Known in Mint State: 700-800 Coins

TOTAL KNOWN BY GRADE			
MS-60 to MS-63	**MS-64**	**MS-65**	**MS-66 or Finer**
300-350 Coins	325-375 Coins	65-75 Coins	6-8 Coins

VALUES BY GRADE			
MS-60	**MS-63**	**MS-65**	**MS-67**
$800-$900	$1,500-$1,750	$7,500-$8,500	--

COLLECTING AND INVESTING STRATEGIES

If you plan to hold out for a fully struck 1927-S you will never be able to purchase an example of this issue. In ten years as a professional numismatist I have never seen a fully struck 1927-S. A much more sound strategy as far as this issue is concerned is to look for a coin with bold-to-sharp striking detail over Liberty's head and the eagle's breast and, most importantly, some measure of separation between the thumb and index finger on Liberty's right (facing) hand. Coins with this degree of striking sharpness do exist – take, for example, the plate coin at the beginning of this section – although they are rare and you are going to have to pass up many coins in your price range before you find a 1927-S that meets these criteria. I truly believe, however, that your patience will be rewarded. Not only will the coin make a more attractive addition to your numismatic holdings, but it will enjoy stronger demand among potential buyers when the time comes to sell.

1928-S

MINTAGE
1,940,000

RARITY RANKINGS

Overall, Mint State: 12th of 65
High Grade, MS-65 or Finer: 16th of 65

EARLY-DATE ISSUES
(1916-1933)

Overall, Mint State: 12th of 26
High Grade, MS-65 or Finer: 16th of 26

Important Varieties: None.

General Comments: The 1928-S is rarer than the 1927-S in terms of total number of Mint State coins known, but it is a bit more plentiful when we consider only those examples that grade MS-65 or finer. In high grades, nonetheless, the 1928-S is still a very rare coin that is more difficult to locate than such other early-date Walking Liberty Half Dollars as the 1916-S, 1918, 1919 and 1933-S.

Strike: A leading strike rarity in this series, the 1928-S almost always displays flat striking detail to Liberty's right (facing) hand on the obverse and the eagle's trailing leg feathers on the reverse. On the other hand, Liberty's head and the eagle's breast feathers are usually bold, if not quite sharp in definition. There are, of course, notable exceptions in the form of examples that are bluntly struck over all four of these design elements.

Luster: The 1928-S has excellent luster that is usually frosty in texture. A small number of coins have more of a satiny sheen, and these are equally as vibrant as the frosty examples.

Surfaces: Expect the typical 1928-S to have scattered abrasions on one or both sides. These features are seldom large in size, but they can be numerous in lower Mint State grades such as MS-62 and MS-63.

Toning: As with the 1927-S, the 1928-S is encountered with light-to-moderate toning almost as often as it is offered with fully brilliant surfaces. The toned examples are seldom spectacular, and the colors are often mottled in distribution and located toward the darker end of the spectrum.

Eye Appeal: This is one of the most divisive issues in the Walking Liberty Half Dollar series as far as eye appeal is concerned. A brilliant, frosty Gem is a genuinely attractive coin despite the fact that the strike will almost certainly be more-or-less soft in the centers. On the other hand, a coin with noticeable abrasions and unattractive toning has no redeeming qualities to offset a soft strike and, hence, will have below-average eye appeal.

Significant Examples:

- **PCGS MS-66.** *Ex: Dallas, TX Signature Auction (Heritage, 11/2005), lot 2178, where it realized $21,275.*
- **NGC MS-66.** *Ex: Santa Clara Elite Coin Auction (Superior, 4/2004), lot 1238, where it realized $10,063; Long Beach Signature Sale (Heritage, 6/2004), lot 6102. The coin did not sell in the Heritage auction.*
- **PCGS MS-66.** *Ex: Nicholas Collection (Heritage, 5/2004), lot 7658, where it realized $25,300.*
- **PCGS MS-66.** *Ex: Ally Collection (Heritage, 7/2002), lot 8531, where it realized $11,500; Long Beach Signature Sale (Heritage, 9/2002), lot 7058. The coin did not sell in the latter auction.*
- **PCGS MS-66.** *Ex: Lindesmith Collection (Bowers and Merena, 3/2000), lot 667, where it realized $10,350.*
- **PCGS MS-66.** *Ex: James Bennett Pryor Collection of United States Half Dollars (Bowers and Merena, 1/1996), lot 354, where it realized $14,300.*

Total Known in Mint State: 475-600 Coins

TOTAL KNOWN BY GRADE			
MS-60 to MS-63	**MS-64**	**MS-65**	**MS-66 or Finer**
200-250 Coins	200-250 Coins	70-80 Coins	8-10 Coins

VALUES BY GRADE			
MS-60	**MS-63**	**MS-65**	**MS-67**
$775-$875	$2,250-$2,750	$9,000-$11,000	--

COLLECTING AND INVESTING STRATEGIES

The best advice that I can offer for the 1928-S is to follow the same strategy that I outlined above for the 1927-S. Namely, look for a coin with bold-to-sharp striking definition over Liberty's head and the eagle's breast as well as a bit of delineation between the thumb and index finger on Liberty's right (facing) hand. I would, however, add one additional caveat for the 1928-S. Insist on acquiring a brilliant coin as the toning found on this issue is often neutral at best and can be distracting when dark in color and/or mottled in distribution.

1929-D

MINTAGE
1,001,200

RARITY RANKINGS

Overall, Mint State: 22nd of 65
High Grade, MS-65 or Finer: 21st of 65

EARLY-DATE ISSUES (1916-1933)

Overall, Mint State: 22nd of 26
High Grade, MS-65 or Finer: 21st of 26

Important Varieties: None.

General Comments: This is the first Half Dollar issue struck in the Denver Mint since 1921. Due to the onset of the Great Depression following the Stock Market Crash of October 29, 1929, many 1929-D Half Dollars were kept from entering circulation immediately after striking. Rather, the coins were retained in federal vaults until the mid-1930s when the worst effects of the Depression had passed. By that time, however, the Philadelphia, Denver and San Francisco Mints had all resumed yearly production of Half Dollars with the result that the 1929-D was largely unnecessary for commercial use. This explains why this issue is much more plentiful in Mint State than a limited original mintage might suggest. In fact, after only the 1916-D, the 1929-D is the second most-common Denver Mint issue in the early Walking Liberty Half Dollar series in all grades from MS-60 through MS-65. The 1929-D is also relatively plentiful in MS-66 when compared to most other Walking Liberty Half Dollars from the 'Teens and '20s. The 1929-D is marginally rarer than the 1929-S in high grades, however, and Gems are also more difficult to obtain than those of the 1916, 1917 and 1933-S. There is only a single Superb Gem 1929-D reported at PCGS and NGC (December/2007).

Strike: The 1929-D is a generally well-struck issue, although a decent number of Mint State examples are softly struck over and around Liberty's right (facing) hand in the center of the obverse. A small percentage of coins are softly defined over Liberty's head and the eagle's breast feathers.

Luster: This is a highly lustrous issue that is usually encountered with thick, rich mint frost.

Surfaces: Mint State 1929-D Half Dollars run the gamut from moderately abraded to virtually pristine, although the average example offered in the market will have a few light bagmarks scattered about.

Toning: Virtually all Mint State examples that I have seen are either fully brilliant with radiant, silver-white surfaces or possess light, iridescent toning. The toned coins tend to be quite attractive, and the most frequently seen colors are gold, tan and silver-gray shades.

Eye Appeal: As a whole, this is an attractive issue.

Significant Examples: A lone PCGS MS-67 is the finest 1929-D Half Dollar listed at the major certification services (December/2007). To the best of my knowledge, this coin has not sold through auction anytime during the eight-year period from 2000-2007.

Total Known in Mint State: 950-1,125 Coins

TOTAL KNOWN BY GRADE			
MS-60 to MS-63	**MS-64**	**MS-65**	**MS-66 or Finer**
350-400 Coins	350-400 Coins	200-250 Coins	55-65 Coins

VALUES BY GRADE			
MS-60	**MS-63**	**MS-65**	**MS-67**
$300-$350	$500-$700	$1,500-$2,500	$15,000-$25,000+

COLLECTING AND INVESTING STRATEGIES

I would not consider acquiring the 1929-D in any grade below the MS-65 level. Gems are offered on a regular basis, and they are usually among the more sharply struck and (definitely) most attractive examples of this issue.

1929-S

MINTAGE
1,902,000

RARITY RANKINGS

Overall, Mint State: 20th of 65
High Grade, MS-65 or Finer: 22nd of 65

EARLY-DATE ISSUES
(1916-1933)

Overall, Mint State: 20th of 26
High Grade, MS-65 or Finer: 22nd of 26

Important Varieties: None.

General Comments: The 1929-S is the most common San Francisco Mint Half Dollar from the 1920s, and it is also one of the most plentiful mintmarked issues in the early Walking Liberty series. The 1929-S, however, is rarer than the 1916, 1916-D, 1917, 1920, 1929-D and 1933-S in terms of total number of Mint State coins known. In high grades, the 1929-S is more difficult to locate than all of these issues with the exception of the 1920 and, perhaps, the 1929-D. There are a few more Superb Gems known for the 1929-S than for the 1929-D, but this San Francisco Mint issue is still a major rarity in MS-67.

Strike: The 1929-S is not the most poorly struck San Francisco Mint Walking Liberty Half Dollar from the 1920s. I have seen many examples that are actually quite bold. Nevertheless, the typical Mint State survivor will have incompleteness of detail over Liberty's right (facing) hand on the obverse and the eagle's trailing leg feathers on the reverse. Liberty's head is also occasionally soft in detail, but the eagle's breast feathers are usually sharp.

Luster: This issue has excellent, usually frosty mint luster.

Surfaces: Scattered abrasions are almost always seen on the surfaces of most Mint State 1929-S Half Dollars. Fortunately, they are usually small in size and limited in number. There are quite a few Gems available, however, and these are expectably smooth for the assigned grade.

Toning: There are a few more toned 1929-S Half Dollars in numismatic circles than there are for the 1929-D. Such examples are seldom heavily toned, however, and they are usually lightly toned throughout or peripherally toned in moderately deep shades. Most Mint State 1929-S Half Dollars that you will encounter in the market, however, are fully brilliant with radiant, frosty-white surfaces.

Eye Appeal: Like the 1929-D, the 1929-S is an aesthetically pleasing issue.

Significant Examples:

- **NGC MS-67.** *Ex: Long Beach Signature Auction (Heritage, 9/2005), lot 3426, where it realized $13,225.*
- **PCGS MS-67.** *Ex: FUN Signature Sale (Heritage, 1/2005), lot 30256, where it realized $71,875.*
- **NGC MS-67.** *Ex: Mandalay Bay Rarities Sale (Bowers and Merena, 10/2004), lot 366. The coin did not sell in that auction.*

Total Known in Mint State: 900-1,075 Coins

TOTAL KNOWN BY GRADE			
MS-60 to MS-63	**MS-64**	**MS-65**	**MS-66 or Finer**
250-300 Coins	500-600 Coins	250-300 Coins	60-70 Coins

VALUES BY GRADE			
MS-60	**MS-63**	**MS-65**	**MS-67**
$300-$350	$500-$700	$1,500-$2,500	$10,000-$20,000+

COLLECTING AND INVESTING STRATEGIES

The 1929-S is often touted as a major strike rarity. This is simply not true. While there are definitely some poorly struck examples out there, even such pieces will seldom be completely smooth in the center of the obverse and/or over Liberty's head. What's more, enough boldly struck examples trade on a yearly basis that you should have little difficulty acquiring one as long as you are willing to wait upward of a few months to make a purchase. Unless the coin in question has full definition that includes good curvature to the bottom of Liberty's right (facing) hand, I would not pay a premium for a 1929-S Half Dollar based solely on striking quality.

1933-S

MINTAGE
1,786,000

RARITY RANKINGS

Overall, Mint State: *23rd of 65*
High Grade, MS-65 or Finer: *23rd of 65*

EARLY-DATE ISSUES
(1916-1933)

Overall, Mint State: *23rd of 26*
High Grade, MS-65 or Finer: *23rd of 26*

Important Varieties: None.

General Comments: The 1933-S is the final issue in the early Walking Liberty Half Dollar series. Despite being the most plentiful San Francisco Mint Half Dollar struck from 1916-1933, the 1933-S is rarer than the 1916, 1916-D and 1917 in all Mint State grades. Although it commands a higher premium, the 1933-S is actually more plentiful, and thus overrated, when compared to the 1929-D and 1929-S. The 1933-S is a legitimately rare issue in MS-66. It is exceedingly so as a Superb Gem.

Strike: This is one of the most consistently well-struck issues in the entire Walking Liberty Half Dollar series, and most examples are at least sharply defined. In fact, there are quite a few fully struck pieces from which to choose. In my years as a numismatic professional, I cannot recall ever handling a 1933-S that was less than boldly defined with at least moderate separation between the thumb and index finger on Liberty's right (facing) hand.

Luster: A lustrous 1933-S is a vibrant, attractive coin that almost always has a richly frosted texture.

Surfaces: This is a well-preserved issue, and even lower-grade Mint State coins usually have only wispy abrasions or, at most, one or two moderate-size bagmarks.

Toning: Most 1933-S Half Dollars that I have seen are either fully brilliant or lightly toned in iridescent shades. Nevertheless, there are a few more moderately-to-deeply toned examples of this issue than there are for the 1929-D and 1929-S. The deeper colors found on this issue are generally pleasing and sometimes quite vivid.

Eye Appeal: Sharp striking detail, excellent luster and above-average surface preservation provide strong eye appeal for most examples of this issue.

Significant Examples:

- **PCGS MS-67.** *Ex: Mid-Winter ANA Signature Sale (Heritage, 3/1999), lot 6483, where it realized $4,485; FUN Signature Sale (Heritage, 1/2000), lot 6897; ANA Charlotte National Money Show Auction (Heritage, 3/2007), lot 1043; Milwaukee, WI ANA Signature Coin Auction (Heritage, 8/2007), lot 1706, where it realized $11,500. The coin did not sell in the March, 2000 and March, 2007 auctions.*

- **NGC MS-67.** *Ex: ANA Charlotte National Money Show Auction (Heritage, 3/2007), lot 1044, where it realized $8,050.*

- **PCGS MS-67.** *Ex: Sounder; FUN Signature Coin Auction (Heritage, 1/2007), lot 1015, where it realized $16,675.*

- **PCGS MS-67.** *Ex: Palm Beach, FL Signature Sale (Heritage, 11/2004), lot 6952, where it realized $14,088; Kallenberg Registry Set of Walking Liberty Half Dollar 1933 to 1947 (Heritage, 11/2005), lot 2699, where it realized $14,950.*

- **PCGS MS-67.** *Ex: Trevor Whitefield Collection (Heritage, 1/2005), lot 30257, where it realized $18,400.*

- **PCGS MS-67.** *Ex: Nicholas Collection (Heritage, 5/2004), lot 7670, where it realized $13,800.*

- **PCGS MS-67.** *Ex: Long Beach Signature Sale (Heritage, 9/2004), lot 6770, where it realized $14,375.*

Total Known in Mint State: 975-1,125 Coins

TOTAL KNOWN BY GRADE			
MS-60 to MS-63	**MS-64**	**MS-65**	**MS-66 or Finer**
350-400 Coins	325-375 Coins	200-250 Coins	90-110 Coins

VALUES BY GRADE			
MS-60	**MS-63**	**MS-65**	**MS-67**
$500-$600	$1,000-$1,200	$2,500-$3,500	$10,000-$20,000

COLLECTING AND INVESTING STRATEGIES

When it comes to the 1933-S, accept nothing less than a sharp strike. I even suggest waiting for the opportunity to purchase an example with a full strike. Such pieces exist in greater quantities than for any of the preceding issues in this series.

If you are looking for only one Walking Liberty Half Dollar for inclusion in a Mint State type set or numismatic portfolio, I would focus on the 1933-S. It is true that the more plentiful issues from the 'Teens and '20s are highly desirable because they were struck during the earliest years of this series. It is also true that most of the later-date issues from 1934-1947 are well-produced, well-preserved and more affordably priced. The 1933-S, however, offers a unique blend of these traits. It is part of the early Walking Liberty Half Dollar series, produced to an uncommonly high standard of quality and is relatively affordable in MS-65 and MS-66.

1934

MINTAGE
6,964,000

RARITY RANKINGS

Overall, Mint State: 39th of 65
High Grade, MS-65 or Finer: 37th of 65

MIDDLE-DATE ISSUES
(1934-1940)

Overall, Mint State: 13th of 19
High Grade, MS-65 or Finer: 11th of 19

Important Varieties: None.

General Comments: The 1934 is obtainable with patience in all grades from MS-60 through MS-66, but it is not the most common middle-date issue in the Walking Liberty Half Dollar series. In fact, the 1934 is rarer than the 1936, 1937, 1939, 1939-D, 1940 and 1940-S in terms of total number of Mint State coins known. MS-67s are scarce in an absolute sense, but the 1934 actually has one of the larger certified populations in this grade for a Walking Liberty Half Dollar. The 1934 is also a relatively obtainable issue in MS-68, although such pieces are decidedly rare when viewed in the wider context of the numismatic market.

Strike: The 1934 usually comes sharply or fully struck, and very few examples have less than bold definition.

Luster: A thick, frosty texture is the norm for this issue, and the quality of the luster is excellent.

Surfaces: The 1934 ranges from moderately abraded to virtually pristine. The typical example is overall smooth with no more than a few wispy abrasions.

Toning: Most examples that I have seen are brilliant or lightly toned.

Eye Appeal: Virtually all 1934 Half Dollars have strong eye appeal either in an absolute sense or, for lower-quality pieces, within the context of the assigned grade.

Significant Examples:

- **PCGS MS-68.** *Ex: Denver ANA Auction (Bowers and Merena, 8/2006), lot 3462, where it realized $6,038; ANA Charlotte National Money Show Auction (Heritage, 3/2007), lot 1045. The coin did not sell in the Heritage auction.*
- **NGC MS-68.** *Ex: ANA Charlotte National Money Show Auction (Heritage, 3/2007), lot 1046, where it realized $2,990.*
- **PCGS MS-68.** *Ex: Anne Kate Collection (Bowers and Merena, 11/2006), lot 3341, where it realized $7,015.*
- **NGC MS-68.** *Ex: CSNS Signature Auction (Heritage, 4/2006), lot 2943, where it realized $5,750.*
- **NGC MS-68.** *Ex: Robert Moreno Collection (Heritage, 7/2005), lot 10028, where it realized $4,025.*
- **PCGS MS-68.** *Ex: Long Beach Signature Sale (Heritage, 2/2003), lot 6964, where it realized $3,565.*

Total Known in Mint State: 3,575-4,175 Coins

TOTAL KNOWN BY GRADE			
MS-60 to MS-63	**MS-64**	**MS-65**	**MS-66 or Finer**
775-875 Coins	1,075-1,275 Coins	1,000-1,200 Coins	725-825 Coins

VALUES BY GRADE			
MS-60	**MS-63**	**MS-65**	**MS-67**
$70-$80	$90-$100	$350-$500	$8,000-$1,000

COLLECTING AND INVESTING STRATEGIES

The 1934 is a well-produced issue with numerous high-quality examples known. You should be very pleased with your acquisition if you select a coin that grades MS-65 or finer.

1934-D

MINTAGE
2,361,000

RARITY RANKINGS

Overall, Mint State: 30th of 65
High Grade, MS-65 or Finer: 30th of 65

MIDDLE-DATE ISSUES
(1934-1940)

Overall, Mint State: 5th of 19
High Grade, MS-65 or Finer: 4th of 19

Important Varieties: None.

General Comments: The 1934-D is the first Half Dollar struck in the Denver Mint since 1929. Although only a median rarity when viewed in the context of the entire Walking Liberty Half Dollar series, the 1934-D is a leading rarity among the middle-date issues struck from 1934-1940. In fact, the 1934-D is the rarest Denver Mint issue in the middle-date Walking Liberty Half Dollar series after only the 1935-D. The 1934-D is also much rarer than the 1939-S in Mint State despite the fact that both issues have similar mintages, and I believe that most examples of the 1934-D were placed into circulation shortly after striking. Still, the 1934-D is obtainable with patience in all grades through MS-64, although MS-65s are moderately scarce and MS-66s are borderline rare. Superb Gems are extremely rare and number just three MS-67s at PCGS and NGC (December/2007).

Strike: The 1934-D is only marginally less well struck than the 1934, and most examples are boldly, if not sharply defined over Liberty's right (facing) hand as well as the eagle's breast and trailing leg feathers. Pay special attention to Liberty's head, however, as it is often a bit soft even if the coin is sharply struck in most other areas.

Luster: This issue has excellent luster, and most examples have thick mint frost.

Surfaces: Most 1934-D Half Dollars are lightly-to-moderately abraded, and even an MS-65 is apt to show one or two wispy bagmarks.

Toning: This issue typically comes brilliant or lightly toned in golden iridescence. A few pieces have deeper toning at the rims, but it is not often that you will encounter an example with moderate-to-heavy toning throughout.

Eye Appeal: The 1934-D has above-average eye appeal and well-struck examples that grade MS-64 or finer are highly attractive.

Significant Examples:

• **NGC MS-67.** *Ex: FUN Signature Auction (Heritage, 1/2006), lot 4052, where it realized $4,088; ANA Charlotte National Money Show Auction (Heritage, 3/2007), lot 1049, where it realized $4,313.*

• **PCGS MS-67.** *Ex: Denver, CO Signature & Platinum Night Auction (Heritage, 8/2006), lot 5271, where it realized $23,000.*

Total Known in Mint State: 2,125-2,525 Coins

TOTAL KNOWN BY GRADE			
MS-60 to MS-63	**MS-64**	**MS-65**	**MS-66 or Finer**
525-625 Coins	975-1,125 Coins	500-600 Coins	125-175 Coins

VALUES BY GRADE			
MS-60	**MS-63**	**MS-65**	**MS-67**
$125-$150	$175-$250	$1,000-$1,500	$5,000-$30,000

COLLECTING AND INVESTING STRATEGIES

Unless you do not mind searching through auctions and dealers' inventories for more than a year, I would accept a bit of striking incompleteness to Liberty's head when it comes to the 1934-D. On the other hand, you can be stricter with the detail over the central highpoints as many examples that I have seen are more-or-less sharp in those areas. Also, be wary of the occasional reeding mark on a coin that has been certified MS-66 by PCGS or NGC. Even though small, these features can detract from the overall eye appeal. Enough MS-66s have been graded that you should be able to find a smooth, pristine-looking example without too much effort.

1934-S

MINTAGE
3,652,000

RARITY RANKINGS

Overall, Mint State: *24th of 65*
High Grade, MS-65 or Finer: *25th of 65*

MIDDLE-DATE ISSUES (1934-1940)

Overall, Mint State: *1st of 19*
High Grade, MS-65 or Finer: *1st of 19*

Important Varieties: None.

General Comments: The 1934-S is the leading rarity among the middle-date Walking Liberty Half Dollars. It is also rarer in most Mint State grades than the 1916, 1916-D and 1917 from the early portion of this series. The typical 1934-S grades no finer than MS-64, although MS-65s trade frequently enough that you should have numerous buying opportunities throughout a normal year of numismatic activity. MS-66s are rare, and there are probably no more than ten Superb Gems known.

Strike: The 1934-S is an interesting issue in that, while it is not among the most poorly struck San Francisco Mint issues in this series, the typical example will still be somewhat deficient in detail on one or both sides. On the obverse, incompleteness of strike is usually more prevalent on Liberty's head than it is over and around the right (facing) hand. On the reverse, the eagle's trailing leg feathers are almost always incomplete, while many examples are also a bit blunt in the center of the breast.

Luster: Luster quality varies for this issue. Most examples are equally as vibrant as the typical 1934 or 1934-D, and these coins tend to have a richly frosted texture. Others are less vibrant with either a satiny or more softly frosted finish.

Surfaces: Most examples are at least lightly abraded, making the 1934-S one of the more challenging Half Dollars produced from 1934-1940 to locate with smooth surfaces.

Toning: Although most 1934-S Half Dollars are brilliant or lightly toned, there are a few more moderately toned examples around than there are for the 1934 and 1934-D. As with the 1934-D, deeper toning for the 1934-S tends to be concentrated in the peripheral areas.

Eye Appeal: Eye appeal for this issue is average to slightly above average. The strike is usually noticeably soft in at least one or two areas, and the typical example will have at least a few distracting abrasions scattered about. The better-looking pieces at any Mint State grade level are usually those with vibrant, frosty luster.

Significant Examples:

• **PCGS MS-67.** *Ex: Robert Moreno Collection (Heritage, 7/2005), lot 10030, where it realized $13,225.*

• **PCGS MS-67.** *Ex: Rarities Sale (Bowers and Merena, 1/2003), lot 374, where it realized $13,800.*

• **PCGS MS-67.** *Ex: Jack Lee; Long Beach Sale (Heritage, 10/2000), lot 6296, where it realized $8,050; Ally Collection (Heritage, 7/2002), lot 8537, where it realized $8,625.*

Total Known in Mint State: 1,100-1,300 Coins

TOTAL KNOWN BY GRADE			
MS-60 to MS-63	MS-64	MS-65	MS-66 or Finer
325-375 Coins	450-500 Coins	235-285 Coins	95-115 Coins

VALUES BY GRADE			
MS-60	MS-63	MS-65	MS-67
$275-$375	$650-$750	$3,500-$4,500	$8,000-$20,000

COLLECTING AND INVESTING STRATEGIES

Many professional numismatists, as well as most collectors and investors, do not consider the 1934-S to be one of the major strike rarities in the Walking Liberty Half Dollar series. While this view is technically correct, there is a noticeable difference in strike between the typically offered example and the handful of truly noteworthy representatives. Most collectors and investors devote their time, energy and much of their financial resources to pursuing the key-date issues and strike rarities in this series such as the 1919-D, 1921-S and 1944-S. The thought here is that attractive, premium-quality examples of these issues will set their collection or portfolio apart from the norm. This is sound reasoning, but the same buyers often settle upon the first 1934-S that they come across in their chosen grade. This is a mistake, since you are also going to have to be highly selective with the 1934-S if you truly want to assemble one of the finest-known Walking Liberty Half Dollar sets. For every ten examples that I have seen with noticeable softness of strike in one or more areas, I have seen only one coin that was sharply struck throughout. And it is that one coin that you should be looking for when building a Walking Liberty Half Dollar set that will be both a pride to own and has the greatest chance of providing a strong return on your investment.

1935

MINTAGE
9,162,000

RARITY
RANKINGS

Overall, Mint State: *38th of 65*
High Grade, MS-65 or Finer: *36th of 65*

MIDDLE-DATE ISSUES
(1934-1940)

Overall, Mint State: *12th of 19*
High Grade, MS-65 or Finer: *10th of 19*

Important Varieties: None.

General Comments: As a high-mintage Philadelphia Mint issue, the 1935 is readily obtainable in all grades from MS-60 through MS-65. The 1935 is still nowhere near as plentiful as the later-date issues in this series from the 1940s, and it is also more challenging to locate than the 1934, 1936, 1937, 1939, 1939-D, 1940 and 1940-S. MS-66s are moderately scarce, and any example that grades MS-67 or MS-68 is a decidedly rare coin.

Strike: The typical 1935 is sharply struck in most areas, but the central obverse highpoint over and before Liberty's right (facing) hand is invariably weak. The feathers on the eagle's trailing leg are also apt to be incomplete.

Luster: The 1935 usually has very good-to-excellent luster. Most examples that I have seen are fully frosted in texture. The occasional satiny piece does turn up, and these tend to be a bit less vibrant in appearance.

Surfaces: Most Mint State examples encountered in the market have a few well-scattered bagmarks, but there are also significant numbers of both moderately abraded and virtually pristine coins among the survivors.

Toning: When present at all, toning on a 1935 Half Dollar is usually light in color with an iridescent quality.

Eye Appeal: As an issue, the 1935 has above-average, if not strong eye appeal.

Significant Examples: In addition to the MS-67s listed below, a single coin certified MS-68 at PCGS also qualifies as a significant example of this issue. I have been unable to locate an auction sale for this coin anytime during the eight-year period from 2000-2007.

- **PCGS MS-67.** *Ex: Kallenberg Registry Set of Walking Liberty Half Dollars 1933 to 1947 (Heritage, 11/2005), lot 2703, where it realized $3,738; Long Beach Signature Auction (Heritage, 6/2006), lot 1822, where it realized $6,325.*
- **PCGS MS-67.** *Ex: CSNS Signature Auction (Heritage, 5/2005), lot 7417, where it realized $3,105; FUN Signature Auction (Heritage, 1/2006), lot 4062, where it realized $2,990.*
- **PCGS MS-67.** *Ex: ANA Sale of the Millennium (Bowers and Merena, 8/2000), lot 4283, where it realized $1,150; Dr. Frank Lanza Collection of Walking Liberty Half Dollars (Heritage, 8/2004), lot 6529, where it realized $4,140.*
- **PCGS MS-67.** *Ex: Santa Clara Signature Sale (Heritage, 11/2002), lot 6211, where it realized $3,105.*
- **PCGS MS-67.** *Ex: Wayne S. Rich Collection (Bowers and Merena, 3/2002), lot 2570, where it realized $1,725.*

Total Known in Mint State: 3,550-4,100 Coins

TOTAL KNOWN BY GRADE			
MS-60 to MS-63	**MS-64**	**MS-65**	**MS-66 or Finer**
650-750 Coins	1,250-1,450 Coins	1,200-1,400 Coins	450-500 Coins

VALUES BY GRADE			
MS-60	**MS-63**	**MS-65**	**MS-67**
$35-$45	$65-$75	$250-$350	$1,500-$3,500+

COLLECTING AND INVESTING STRATEGIES

Since this is a generally well-produced issue with a sizeable population at and above the MS-65 grade level, you should have very little difficulty finding an attractive example for inclusion in your collection or portfolio. Be prepared to accept some softness of detail over the central obverse highpoint, but patience will be rewarded with a sharp strike on the reverse that also extends to the innermost feathers on the eagle's trailing leg. One other caveat – avoid satiny examples. Coins with this finish are in the minority among surviving 1935 Half Dollars, but those that I have seen tend to have a subdued, almost lackluster appearance.

1935-D

MINTAGE
3,003,800

RARITY
RANKINGS

Overall, Mint State: *28th of 65*
High Grade, MS-65 or Finer: *29th of 65*

MIDDLE-DATE ISSUES
(1934-1940)

Overall, Mint State: *3rd of 19*
High Grade, MS-65 or Finer: *3rd of 19*

Important Varieties: None.

General Comments: The 1935-D is one of the scarcer Walking Liberty Half Dollars, and it is the rarest Denver Mint issue from the middle portion of the series. Most examples grade no finer than MS-64. MS-65s are moderately scarce, MS-66s rare and Superb Gems unknown.

Strike: The typical example is in the softly struck category, and even a boldly struck 1935-D with the slightest separation between the thumb and index finger on Liberty's right (facing) hand is noteworthy. In addition, Liberty's head is always softly struck to at least some degree, and many coins are quite blunt in that area. The reverse is definitely the better struck of the two sides, and it seldom has bothersome lack of detail over the eagle's breast, although the trailing leg feathers are often less-than-complete.

Luster: Bright, frosty luster is commonplace on Mint State 1935-D Half Dollars.

Surfaces: Unfortunately, scattered abrasions are seen quite often on survivors of this issue. Very rare is the 1935-S that approaches perfection in terms of surface preservation. There are, however, enough MS-65s available that you should be able to procure an overall smooth-looking example given enough time and sufficient financial resources.

Toning: Like the 1934-dated issues and the 1935, the 1935-D is almost always encountered with either brilliant surfaces or light, iridescent toning. Moderate and deep colors, when present, are usually confined to the peripheries on one or both sides.

Eye Appeal: Overall eye appeal for this issue is only average. Vibrant luster and bright surfaces are positive attributes, but soft striking detail and noticeable abrasions are detracting features. High-grade coins with overall smooth surfaces, however, have above-average eye appeal.

Significant Examples:

- **PCGS MS-66.** *Ex: Summer FUN Signature Coin Auction (Heritage, 7/2007), lot 1042, where it realized $3,881.*

- **PCGS MS-66.** *Ex: FUN Signature Coin Auction (Heritage, 1/2007), lot 4745; Dallas, TX Signature Coin Auction (Heritage, 4/2007), lot 844, where it realized $3,960. The coin did not sell in the first-listed auction.*

- **PCGS MS-66.** *Ex: Baltimore Auction (Bowers and Merena, 3/2006), lot 1460, where it realized $8,050.*

- **PCGS MS-66.** *Ex: Pre-Long Beach Sale (Ira & Larry Goldberg, 5/2004), lot 749, where it realized $8,050.*

- **PCGS MS-66.** *Ex: Jackson Sale (Kingswood, 8/2002), lot 1497, where it realized $5,290.*

- **PCGS MS-66.** *Ex: Wayne S. Rich Collection (Bowers and Merena, 3/2002), lot 2571, where it realized $8,050.*

Total Known in Mint State: 1,650-1,850 Coins

TOTAL KNOWN BY GRADE			
MS-60 to MS-63	**MS-64**	**MS-65**	**MS-66 or Finer**
385-435 Coins	750-850 Coins	450-500 Coins	70-80 Coins

VALUES BY GRADE			
MS-60	**MS-63**	**MS-65**	**MS-67**
$100-$150	$200-$300	$1,500-$2,500	--

COLLECTING AND INVESTING STRATEGIES

Do not be obsessed with finding a fully struck 1935-D, for I am convinced that no such coin exists. Instead, acquire a coin that has been graded MS-66 by one of the two leading certification services. Both PCGS and NGC take strike into account when grading Walking Liberty Half Dollars, and a 1935-D in MS-66 will have above-average definition over Liberty's head and right (facing) hand. Such a coin will also be free of the distracting abrasions that almost always accompany lower-grade Mint State examples (even many of those that grade MS-65).

1935-S

MINTAGE
3,854,000

RARITY RANKINGS

Overall, Mint State: 25th of 65
High Grade, MS-65 or Finer: 27th of 65

MIDDLE-DATE ISSUES
(1934-1940)

Overall, Mint State: 2nd of 19
High Grade, MS-65 or Finer: 2nd of 19

Important Varieties: None.

General Comments: After only the 1934-S, the 1935-S is the rarest Walking Liberty Half Dollar struck from 1934 through 1940. MS-64 is the highest grade that is available with any degree of regularity, and you will almost certainly have to exercise considerable patience for the opportunity to purchase an MS-65. The 1935-S is rare in MS-66 and exceedingly so in MS-67.

Strike: Most 1935-S Half Dollars are not going to win any awards for striking quality. Expect to see lack of detail over Liberty's head and right (facing) hand, as well as on the eagle's trailing leg feathers. The eagle's breast sometimes lacks full feather definition. That said, there are a surprising number of coins out there with emerging, if not downright bold definition in one or more of these areas. Cherrypicking will definitely be rewarded with an above-average example.

Luster: The 1935-S usually has excellent, fully frosted luster.

Surfaces: With most Mint State coins grading MS-64 or lower, the 1935-S usually displays at least a few noticeable abrasions.

Toning: Most 1935-S Half Dollars are brilliant, although a lightly toned example is encountered now and then.

Eye Appeal: The 1935-S is similar in striking quality and surface preservation to the 1935-D. It also merits only an average rating in the area of eye appeal. The few premium-quality Gems and Superb Gems that have survived, however, are very attractive.

Significant Examples:

• **PCGS MS-67.** *Ex: Palm Beach, FL Signature Sale (Heritage, 11/2004), lot 6569, where it realized $21,275.*

Total Known in Mint State: 1,250-1,475 Coins

TOTAL KNOWN BY GRADE			
MS-60 to MS-63	**MS-64**	**MS-65**	**MS-66 or Finer**
250-300 Coins	550-650 Coins	350-400 Coins	100-125 Coins

VALUES BY GRADE			
MS-60	**MS-63**	**MS-65**	**MS-67**
$200-$300	$350-$450	$2,000-$3,000	$8,000-$20,000+

COLLECTING AND INVESTING STRATEGIES

Your best chance for avoiding the soft striking detail and noticeably abraded surfaces for which this issue is known is to purchase a coin that grades MS-66. MS-67s are even more desirable, of course, but they are worth upward of 2.5 times more than an MS-66 if graded by NGC. A PCGS MS-67 will set you back at least $20,000 due to pressure from Registry Set collectors. At $3,000-$5,000, therefore, a 1935-S that grades MS-66 offers strong technical quality and eye appeal for the issue at a much more affordable price.

Proof
1936

MINTAGE
3,901

RARITY
RANKINGS

Overall, All Proof Grades: 1st of 7
High Grade, Proof-65 or Finer: 1st of 7

Important Varieties: None.

General Comments: The 1936 is the first issue in the proof Walking Liberty Half Dollar series, and it is also the rarest. This is a well-preserved issue, however, with most survivors grading Proof-64 through Proof-66. Superb Gems, though quite rare, include a stunning Proof-68 certified at PCGS (December/2007).

Strike: Virtually all examples are fully struck with razor-sharp definition that extends to the finest elements of Liberty's right (facing) hand and the innermost feathers on the eagle's trailing leg. Every once in a while an example will turn up that is a tad soft in one or both of these areas, although the lack of detail will be minor and anything but distracting.

Finish: The Mint used all-brilliant proofing techniques to produce this issue and, as a result, most examples have a bright, mirrored finished both in the fields and over the devices. I have seen a very small number of coins with the lightest bit of mint frost over Liberty's portrait on the obverse and the reverse eagle. None of these pieces, however, have enough contrast between the fields and devices to warrant a Cameo designation from one of the two leading certification services.

Surfaces: The typical proof 1936 is well preserved with overall smooth, if not virtually pristine surfaces.

Toning: Most examples are fully brilliant or only lightly toned, although there are enough moderately toned examples that these are encountered on a fairly regular basis. The toned coins are seldom vivid, and the most prevalent colors are hazy-silver, golden-tan, orange-copper and russet shades. Generally speaking, the deeper, more vivid colors are confined to the rims.

Eye Appeal: As an issue, the proof 1936 has very strong eye appeal.

Significant Examples:

• **PCGS Proof-68.** *Ex: Nicholas Collection (Heritage, 5/2004), lot 7818, where it realized $74,750; Bruce Scher #1 All-Time PCGS Registry Set (Heritage, 2/2005), lot 4132, where it realized $80,500.*

• **NGC Proof-67.** *Ex: Baltimore Auction (Bowers and Merena, 11/2007), lot 2355; Orlando Rarities Sale (Bowers and Merena, 1/2008), lot 263, where it realized $8,913. The coin did not sell in the first-listed auction.*

• **NGC Proof-67.** *Ex: Pre-Long Beach Rarities Sale (Bowers and Merena, 2/2007), lot 389, where it realized $8,625.*

• **PCGS Proof-67.** *Ex: Palm Beach, FL Signature Auction (Heritage, 3/2006), lot 1578, where it realized $23,000.*

• **PCGS Proof-67.** *Ex: FUN Signature Auction (Heritage, 1/2006), lot 3212, where it realized $29,900.*

• **NGC Proof-67★.** *Ex: Dallas, TX Signature Auction (Heritage, 11/2005), lot 2180, where it realized $16,100.*

Total Known: 1,600-1,850 Coins

TOTAL KNOWN BY GRADE			
Proof-60 to Proof-63	Proof-64	Proof-65	Proof-66 or Finer
240-290 Coins	525-625 Coins	450-500 Coins	385-435 Coins

VALUES BY GRADE			
Proof-60	Proof-63	Proof-65	Proof-67
$825-$925	$2,500-$3,500	$4,000-$5,500	$10,000-$30,000

COLLECTING AND INVESTING STRATEGIES

In my opinion, the most attractive and, hence, desirable proof 1936 Walking Liberty Half Dollars are those that are free of dark and/or hazy toning. Since most originally toned examples tend to have dark, mottled patina at the rims and/or hazy overtones toward the centers, I suggest acquiring one of the brilliant specimens that are available in the market. If you have a preference for toned coins, look for one of the few proof 1936 Half Dollars with vivid red or orange colors. (The plate coin at the beginning of this section is an excellent example of such a coin.) Chances are that these colors will be confined to the rims. If this is the case, make sure that the centers are bright and free of overly hazy silver or golden-tan patina that can subdue the underlying brilliant finish.

1936

MINTAGE
12,614,000

RARITY RANKINGS

Overall, Mint State: *43rd of 65*
High Grade, MS-65 or Finer: *47th of 65*

MIDDLE-DATE ISSUES
(1934-1940)

Overall, Mint State: *17th of 19*
High Grade, MS-65 or Finer: *17th of 19*

Important Varieties: Two Doubled Die Obverse varieties are known. FS-101 is by far the more visually dramatic. It is also much rarer than the variety that is attributed alternatively as FS-102 and Fox V-101. The latter variety is due to doubling in a master die.

General Comments: The 1936 is more common than any of the preceding issues in the Walking Liberty Half Dollar series, but it is not quite as plentiful as the 1939 and 1940, to say nothing of most later-date issues from 1941-1947. Examples are readily obtainable in all grades up to and including MS-66. MS-67s, while scarce in an absolute sense, are still relatively plentiful by the standards of this series. A few MS-68s are known, but the 1936 is clearly very rare at that grade level.

Strike: The 1936 is usually sharply struck with good-to-excellent detail in and around the centers on both sides.

Luster: Luster for this issue is almost universally excellent. The vast majority of coins have frosty luster.

Surfaces: Although surface preservation for this issue varies widely, it is not at all difficult to locate a minimally abraded, smooth-looking coin.

Toning: Toned examples are in the minority among Mint State 1936 Half Dollars, and such coins tend to have only light, iridescent overtones.

Eye Appeal: This is an attractive issue with a high eye appeal rating.

Significant Examples:

• **NGC MS-68.** *Ex: ANA Charlotte National Money Show Auction (Heritage, 3/2007), lot 1065, where it realized $4,600.*

• **NGC MS-68.** *Ex: Long Beach Signature Sale (Heritage, 2/2005), lot 8042; Dallas, TX Signature Auction (Heritage, 11/2005), lot 2828, where it realized $5,463. The coin did not sell in the first-listed auction.*

• **NGC MS-68.** *Ex: FUN Signature Sale (Heritage, 1/2001), lot 7863, where it realized $2,415; Long Beach Signature Sale (Heritage, 9/2004), lot 6787, where it realized $4,715.*

Total Known in Mint State: 5,600-6,600+ Coins

TOTAL KNOWN BY GRADE			
MS-60 to MS-63	**MS-64**	**MS-65**	**MS-66 or Finer**
700-800+ Coins	1,700-1,900 Coins	2,100-2,600 Coins	1,100-1,300 Coins

VALUES BY GRADE			
MS-60	**MS-63**	**MS-65**	**MS-67**
$30-$40	$50-$60	$200-$250	$700-$1,000

COLLECTING AND INVESTING STRATEGIES

A Gem or Superb Gem 1936 would make a lovely, yet relatively affordable addition to a high-grade type set. If your numismatic budget is more limited, you can still find a sharply struck, lustrous 1936 with a minimal number of wispy abrasions in MS-63 or MS-64 without too much effort.

1936-D

MINTAGE
4,252,400

RARITY RANKINGS

Overall, Mint State: 35th of 65
High Grade, MS-65 or Finer: 35th of 65

MIDDLE-DATE ISSUES
(1934-1940)

Overall, Mint State: 9th of 19
High Grade, MS-65 or Finer: 9th of 19

Important Varieties: None.

General Comments: The 1936-D is a median rarity among the Walking Liberty Half Dollars produced from 1934 through 1940. Nevertheless, you should have little difficulty locating an example that falls into the MS-60 to MS-65 grade range. Even MS-66s are only moderately scarce. Superb Gems, however, are rare. In high grades, the 1936-D is rarer than such other middle-date issues in this series as the 1939-D, 1939-S and 1940-S.

Strike: Striking quality for this issue ranges from full to a bit soft. Most examples are sharply struck and, when present, incompleteness of detail is usually minor and confined to Liberty's right (facing) hand.

Luster: Vibrant, frosty luster characterizes virtually all Mint State 1936-D Half Dollars with the notable exception of lower-grade, cleaned or overly dipped examples where the original mint finish has been impaired.

Surfaces: The typical 1936-D will be a bit more noticeably abraded than most 1936 Half Dollars. Consequently, it is more difficult to locate a 1936-D with overall smooth or virtually pristine surfaces.

Toning: If you are a fan of richly toned silver coins, the 1936-D Walking Liberty Half Dollar will be a frustrating issue for you to collect. Most examples are brilliant, and those that are not are seldom more than lightly toned in iridescent silver, gold or similar shades.

Eye Appeal: Eye appeal is well above average for this issue, and high-grade examples are very attractive.

Significant Examples:

- **NGC MS-67.** *Ex: Long Beach, CA Signature U.S. Coin Auction (Heritage, 5/2007), lot 1216, where it realized $4,313.*
- **PCGS MS-67.** *Ex: Anne Kate Collection (Bowers and Merena, 11/2006), lot 3366, where it realized $6,038.*
- **PCGS MS-67.** *Ex: Big Tex Registry Set of Walking Liberty Halves (Heritage, 9/2006), lot 2137, where it realized $5,750.*
- **PCGS MS-67.** *Ex: Denver ANA Auction (Bowers and Merena, 8/2006), lot 3478, where it realized $5,750.*
- **PCGS MS-67.** *Ex: Pre-Long Beach Elite Coin Auction (Superior, 5/2003), lot 2670, where it realized $5,750; Robert Moreno Collection (Heritage, 7/2005), lot 10035, where it realized $6,038; FUN Signature Auction (Heritage, 1/2006), lot 4068, where it realized $6,900.*
- **NGC MS-67.** *Ex: Pre-Long Beach Sale (Superior, 2/2000), lot 357, where it realized $2,645.*

Total Known in Mint State: 3,125-3,625 Coins

TOTAL KNOWN BY GRADE			
MS-60 to MS-63	**MS-64**	**MS-65**	**MS-66 or Finer**
450-500 Coins	1,125-1,325 Coins	1,125-1,325 Coins	425-475 Coins

VALUES BY GRADE			
MS-60	**MS-63**	**MS-65**	**MS-67**
$60-$70	$85-$115	$450-$575	$4,250-$6,750

COLLECTING AND INVESTING STRATEGIES

As with the 1936, you should have no difficulty locating a sharply struck, attractive 1936-D for inclusion among your numismatic holdings. My personal preference is for fully brilliant examples as a lack of toning allows ready appreciation of the vibrant, frosty luster for which this issue is known. I would be remiss if I did not write that the lightly toned examples also tend to be highly attractive coins.

1936-S

MINTAGE
3,884,000

RARITY RANKINGS

Overall, Mint State: 29th of 65
High Grade, MS-65 or Finer: 31st of 65

MIDDLE-DATE ISSUES
(1934-1940)

Overall, Mint State: 4th of 19
High Grade, MS-65 or Finer: 5th of 19

Important Varieties: None.

General Comments: More plentiful than any of the preceding San Francisco Mint Walking Liberty Half Dollars, the 1936-S is still a median rarity when viewed in the context of this entire series. Coins that grade MS-60 to MS-65 should not prove all that difficult to locate, but the 1936-S is not as plentiful in these grades as the 1937-S, 1939-S or 1940-S. MS-66s are scarce by any reckoning, and Superb Gems probably number fewer than 15 coins.

Strike: As a Walking Liberty Half Dollar produced in the San Francisco Mint, it should come as no surprise to read that the 1936-S usually comes with noticeable softness of strike. On the obverse, Liberty's head and right (facing) hand are the areas where you should expect to see at least some lack of detail. On the reverse, the eagle's trailing leg feathers are usually incomplete. On the other hand, the 1936-S is far from the worst-struck issue in the Walking Liberty Half Dollar series, and I have even seen quite a few examples that really are sharply struck. Here is another issue for which Cherrypicking will pay dividends in the area of striking quality.

Luster: This is a highly lustrous issue that almost always displays a vibrant, frosty mint finish.

Surfaces: The typical 1936-S has at least a few scattered abrasions, although these are usually small in size and singularly inconspicuous. Coins that approach perfection in terms of surface preservation are quite rare from a market availability standpoint.

Toning: Brilliant surfaces or light, iridescent toning characterizes most Mint State examples of this issue.

Eye Appeal: Although the typical example will be somewhat softly defined in a few isolated areas, the 1936-S still has above-average eye appeal. This is particularly true in Mint State grades from MS-64 where wispy abrasions will be minimal in number, if not virtually absent.

Significant Examples:

• **NGC MS-67.** *Ex: Palm Beach, FL Signature Sale (Heritage, 11/2004), lot 6974, where it realized $4,140; ANA Charlotte National Money Show Auction (Heritage, 3/2007), lot 1070, where it realized $3,220.*

• **NGC MS-67.** *Ex: Robert Moreno Collection (Heritage, 7/2005), lot 10036, where it realized $3,220; ANA Charlotte National Money Show Auction (Heritage, 3/2007), lot 1071, where it realized $2,760.*

• **PCGS MS-67.** *Ex: Anne Kate Collection (Bowers and Merena, 11/2006), lot 3370, where it realized $17,825.*

• **NGC MS-67.** *Ex: Dallas Signature Coin Auction (Heritage, 10/2006), lot 2097, where it realized $2,990.*

• **NGC MS-67.** *Ex: Long Beach Signature Auction (Heritage, 6/2006), lot 1843, where it realized $3,220; Long Beach, CA Signature Auction (Heritage, 9/2006), lot 2142, where it realized $3,220.*

• **NGC MS-67.** *Ex: Santa Clara Bullet Sale (Heritage, 4/2000), lot 220, where it realized $2,300.*

Total Known in Mint State: 2,150-2,475 Coins

TOTAL KNOWN BY GRADE			
MS-60 to MS-63	**MS-64**	**MS-65**	**MS-66 or Finer**
250-300 Coins	800-900 Coins	835-935 Coins	275-325 Coins

VALUES BY GRADE			
MS-60	**MS-63**	**MS-65**	**MS-67**
$100-$125	$150-$225	$625-$800	$2,750-$8,000

COLLECTING AND INVESTING STRATEGIES

As previously stated, Cherrypicking will pay dividends for the 1936-S in the area of striking quality. Be sure to check both Liberty's head and right (facing) hand before making a purchase. I have seen quite a few coins that are sharply struck over and around the right (facing) hand but still quite blunt at Liberty's head. I would not classify a 1936-S as having above-average striking detail for the issue unless it was sharply impressed in both areas.

Proof

1937

MINTAGE
5,728

RARITY RANKINGS

Overall, All Proof Grades: 2nd of 7
High Grade, Proof-65 or Finer: 2nd of 7

Important Varieties: None.

General Comments: After the 1936, the second-year 1937 is the rarest issue in the proof Walking Liberty Half Dollar series. The most significant difference between the two issues in terms of availability does not arise until we get to the Superb Gem grade level. The 1937 is much more available in Proof-67 than the 1936, although it is still somewhat scarce in that grade when viewed in the wider context of the proof Walking Liberty Half Dollar series. The 1937 is rare in Proof-68 and unknown any finer.

Strike: The proof 1937 is almost always fully struck, and I cannot recall ever seeing an example that was less than sharply defined.

Finish: In keeping with the techniques that the Mint used to produce this issue, the proof 1937 usually displays an all-brilliant finish. There are a few coins, however, on which the central devices reveal a bit of light mint frost. The degree of contrast that these coins display is insufficient to secure a Cameo designation from PCGS and NGC.

Surfaces: The typical proof 1937 is a well-preserved coin with few, if any noticeable hairlines or contact marks.

Toning: The vast majority of proof 1937 Half Dollars are at least peripherally toned, and many examples are toned throughout. This issue usually displays gold, tan and/or silver colors that can obscure the underlying mint finish if they have a hazy quality. The more attractively toned examples have rich reddish-russet, orange-russet or soft powder-blue patina that is often confined to the peripheral areas.

Eye Appeal: Examples with moderate toning tend to be below average in eye appeal, but the more lightly toned specimens (as well as the few pieces that are fully brilliant) are usually quite attractive.

Significant Examples: Proof-68 is the highest grade obtainable in a PCGS or NGC-certified proof 1937 Walking Liberty Half Dollar. Such examples include:

- **NGC Proof-68.** Ex: Vanek Collection (Heritage, 7/2007), lot 1096, where it realized $6,325.
- **NGC Proof-68.** Ex: Baltimore Auction (Bowers and Merena, 3/2006), lot 1483, where it realized $4,600.
- **NGC Proof-68.** Ex: San Francisco, CA ANA Signature Auction (Heritage, 7/2005), lot 6456, where it realized $4,888.
- **PCGS Proof-68.** Ex: Robert Moreno Collection (Heritage, 7/2005), lot 10071, where it realized $7,475.
- **PCGS Proof-68.** Ex: Bruce Scher #1 All-Time PCGS Registry Set (Heritage, 2/2005), lot 4133, where it realized $9,775.
- **NGC Proof-68★.** Ex: Pittsburgh, PA Signature Sale (Heritage, 8/2004), lot 6627; FUN Signature Sale (Heritage, 1/2005), lot 7880, where it realized $7,475. The coin did not sell in the first-listed auction.

Total Known: 2,000-2,350 Coins

TOTAL KNOWN BY GRADE			
Proof-60 to Proof-63	Proof-64	Proof-65	Proof-66 or Finer
215-265 Coins	535-635 Coins	525-625 Coins	725-825 Coins

VALUES BY GRADE			
Proof-60	Proof-63	Proof-65	Proof-67
$375-$425	$525-$725	$900-$1,250	$1,750-$3,250

COLLECTING AND INVESTING STRATEGIES

The prevalence of hazy toning among surviving proof 1937 Half Dollars can make it difficult to acquire an attractive example of this issue. If you cannot find a brilliant coin, buy one of the more lightly toned specimens where the underlying mint finish is still vibrant. I also like those toned examples that have vivid colors at the rims on one or both sides, particularly if the centers are bright and free of hazy overtones.

1937

MINTAGE
9,522,000

RARITY RANKINGS

Overall, Mint State: *40th of 65*
High Grade, MS-65 or Finer: *40th of 65*

MIDDLE-DATE ISSUES
(1934-1940)

Overall, Mint State: *14th of 19*
High Grade, MS-65 or Finer: *14th of 19*

Important Varieties: None.

General Comments: Not quite as common as the 1936, 1939 or 1940, the 1937 is still one of the easier middle-date Walking Liberty Half Dollars to locate in all Mint State grades. Examples that grade MS-60 to MS-65 are plentiful, and enough MS-66s exist that you should also not have too much difficulty locating a coin at that level of preservation. A 1937 that grades MS-67 is a rare coin, however, and there are fewer than five MS-68s known.

Strike: This is a high-mintage issue, and striking quality among Mint State survivors varies to a certain degree. Most examples are at least sharply struck, however, and even the more poorly defined coins will have at least emerging definition in the center of the obverse.

Luster: The 1937 has excellent, usually frosty luster.

Surfaces: This is definitely one of the easier Walking Liberty Half Dollars from the 1930s to locate with overall smooth surfaces as defined by the MS-65 grade level. Virtually pristine MS-66s and MS-67s are also relatively easy to come by, especially when the 1937 is compared to most of the earlier-dated issues in this series.

Toning: There are a few more moderately toned examples of the 1937 in the market than there are for the 1936. On these coins, the toning is usually confined to the peripheries. Nevertheless, the typical 1937 is brilliant or lightly toned in iridescent shades.

Eye Appeal: Eye appeal for the 1937 is very strong, and I cannot recall ever having seen a problem-free coin that was unattractive within the context of the assigned grade.

Significant Examples:

• **PCGS MS-68.** *Ex: Anne Kate Collection (Bowers and Merena, 11/2006), lot 3377, where it realized $46,575.*

• **NGC MS-68★.** *Ex: Robert Moreno Collection (Heritage, 7/2005), lot 10037, where it realized $13,800.*

• **PCGS MS-68.** *Ex: Jack Lee; Paul S. Mory, Sr. Collection (Bowers and Merena, 6/2000), lot 532, where it realized $2,588.*

Total Known in Mint State: 4,850-5,450+ Coins

TOTAL KNOWN BY GRADE			
MS-60 to MS-63	**MS-64**	**MS-65**	**MS-66 or Finer**
675-775+ Coins	1,625-1,825 Coins	1,725-1,925 Coins	825-925 Coins

VALUES BY GRADE			
MS-60	**MS-63**	**MS-65**	**MS-67**
$30-$40	$55-$65	$225-$275	$875-$1,100

COLLECTING AND INVESTING STRATEGIES

This is a well-produced, generally well-preserved issue with a sizeable number of Mint State survivors from which to choose. As such, there is little advice I can provide other than to be sure that you are 100% satisfied with the coin in question before you make a purchase. If you do not like a particular 1937 Half Dollar, rest assured that another example in that grade will become available within a very short period of time. The only exception here are coins certified MS-68 by PCGS and NGC. These are so rare that I would not hesitate to acquire an example that becomes available. This is particularly sound advice if you are assembling a top-ranked Registry Set.

1937-D

MINTAGE
1,676,000

**RARITY
RANKINGS**

Overall, Mint State: 31st of 65
High Grade, MS-65 or Finer: 32nd of 65

**MIDDLE-DATE ISSUES
(1934-1940)**

Overall, Mint State: 6th of 19
High Grade, MS-65 or Finer: 6th of 19

Important Varieties: None.

General Comments: For many years in the Walking Liberty Half Dollar series, the Denver Mint issue is more plentiful than the San Francisco Mint issue. This is definitely not the case for the 1937-D and 1937-S. The 1937-D is the rarer coin in all but the lowest *circulated* grades. The 1937-D is also rarer in Mint State than the low-mintage, key-date 1938-D, as well as the 1936-D and 1939-D in high grades. Even examples in the MS-60 to MS-65 grade range are scarce from a market availability standpoint. An MS-66 is a scarce coin by any definition, and Superb Gems are quite rare.

Strike: The 1937-D is seldom offered with 100% full striking detail, but it is still a relatively well-produced issue. The typical example is actually quite sharply defined and, when present, lack of detail is usually minor and confined to Liberty's head, right (facing) hand and/or the eagle's trailing leg feathers.

Luster: Vibrant, frosty mint luster contributes significantly to the overall eye appeal rating of this issue.

Surfaces: Most Mint State 1937-D Half Dollars that I have handled have at least a few scattered abrasions, and even examples that are smooth in most areas are scarce from a market availability standpoint.

Toning: I have seen numerous 1937-D Half Dollars that are brilliant, but also a decent number of coins with light-to-moderate toning. This is one of the more attractive business strikes in this series in terms of toning, and the colors that are present tend to be quite pleasing, if not downright vivid. This is equally true of lightly toned examples as it is for coins with more extensive patination.

Eye Appeal: As a whole, the 1937-D is an attractive issue with above-average, if not strong eye appeal.

Significant Examples:

• **NGC MS-68.** *Ex: New York, NY Signature Sale (Heritage, 7/2002), lot 8612; Robert Moreno Collection (Heritage, 7/2005), lot 10038, where it realized $18,400; FUN Signature Coin Auction (Heritage, 1/2007), lot 1016, where it realized $23,000; Summer FUN Signature Coin Auction (Heritage, 7/2007), lot 1051. The coin did not sell in the first and final-listed auctions.*

Total Known in Mint State: 2,185-2,485 Coins

TOTAL KNOWN BY GRADE			
MS-60 to MS-63	**MS-64**	**MS-65**	**MS-66 or Finer**
380-430 Coins	675-775 Coins	750-850 Coins	380-430 Coins

VALUES BY GRADE			
MS-60	**MS-63**	**MS-65**	**MS-67**
$175-$225	$250-$300	$600-$800	$2,000-$4,000

COLLECTING AND INVESTING STRATEGIES

Be wary of coins with excessive bluntness of detail over Liberty's head and right (facing) hand. These are in the minority among Mint State 1937-D Half Dollars. I would definitely avoid them in favor of a more sharply struck coin.

The 1937-D is one of the few issues in the Walking Liberty Half Dollar series that I would recommend to the toning enthusiast. Even if you are assembling a mostly brilliant set but would like a few examples to represent toning on Half Dollars of this type, the 1937-D is definitely one of your better bets for finding a colorful coin.

1937-S

MINTAGE
2,090,000

RARITY RANKINGS
Overall, Mint State: 33rd of 65
High Grade, MS-65 or Finer: 34th of 65

MIDDLE-DATE ISSUES
(1934-1940)
Overall, Mint State: 8th of 19
High Grade, MS-65 or Finer: 8th of 19

Important Varieties: None.

General Comments: One of the rarer middle-date issues in this series, the 1937-S is more difficult to locate in all Mint State grades than the 1936-D, 1939-D, 1939-S and 1940-S, as well as the Philadelphia Mint issues from 1934-1940. The typical Mint State example falls somewhere in the MS-60 to MS-65 grade range. The 1937-S is scarce in MS-66 and rare as a Superb Gem.

Strike: The typical example is a bit softly struck over and around Liberty's right (facing) hand in the center of the obverse. More often than not, the reverse will also show incompleteness of detail inside the eagle's trailing leg. On the other hand, Liberty's head is usually well defined and, if there is softness of detail in that area, it tends to be minor and not all that distracting to the naked eye.

Luster: The 1937-S has excellent luster that is almost always frosty in texture.

Surfaces: This is a generally well-preserved issue, and the typical example has fewer abrasions than the 1937 and 1937-D.

Toning: A moderately toned coin is a rarity for the 1937-S, and the issue is almost always encountered with brilliant or lightly toned surfaces. The few coins that I have seen with more extensive toning tend to have darker colors with a splotchy distribution that is not particularly attractive.

Eye Appeal: The 1937-S has above-average eye appeal.

Significant Examples:

- **PCGS MS-67.** *Ex: Denver ANA Auction (Bowers and Merena, 8/2006), lot 3491, where it realized $6,670; ANA Charlotte National Money Show Auction (Heritage, 3/2007), lot 1081. The coin did not sell in the Heritage auction.*
- **PCGS MS-67.** *Ex: Baltimore Auction (Bowers and Merena, 3/2006), lot 1484; Denver, CO Signature & Platinum Night Auction (Heritage, 8/2006), lot 3516, where it realized $6,900; ANA Charlotte National Money Show Auction (Heritage, 3/2007), lot 1080, where it realized $4,313. The coin did not sell in the Bowers and Merena auction.*
- **PCGS MS-67.** *Ex: Anne Kate Collection (Bowers and Merena, 11/2006), lot 3386, where it realized $3,738.*
- **NGC MS-67.** *Ex: Robert Moreno Collection (Heritage, 7/2005), lot 10039, where it realized $4,485; ANA Charlotte National Money Show Auction (Heritage, 3/2007), lot 1082, where it realized $3,738.*
- **NGC MS-67.** *Ex: Dallas Signature Coin Auction (Heritage, 11/2006), lot 966, where it realized $4,600.*
- **PCGS MS-67.** *Ex: G B W; Kallenberg Registry Set of Walking Liberty Half Dollars 1933 to 1947 (Heritage, 11/2005), lot 2711, where it realized $8,050; CSNS Signature Auction (Heritage, 4/2006), lot 2969, where it realized $13,800.*

Total Known in Mint State: 2,335-2,635 Coins

TOTAL KNOWN BY GRADE			
MS-60 to MS-63	**MS-64**	**MS-65**	**MS-66 or Finer**
325-375 Coins	800-900 Coins	875-975 Coins	335-385 Coins

VALUES BY GRADE			
MS-60	**MS-63**	**MS-65**	**MS-67**
$125-$150	$150-$200	$575-$750	$3,500-$8,500+

COLLECTING AND INVESTING STRATEGIES

The most highly desirable 1937-S Half Dollars are those that possess above-average striking detail over and around Liberty's right (facing) hand. Such examples are actually quite sharp in that area, and they tend to be concentrated at the MS-66 and MS-67 levels where strike is a significant component of the grade for Walking Liberty Half Dollars.

If your budget precludes acquiring an example of this issue that grades that high, do not lose hope. The occasional sharply struck example does turn up in an MS-63, MS-64 or MS-65 holder. Given the solid technical merits that this issue possesses in areas other than strike, a coin that grades MS-63 to MS-65 will almost certainly have strong eye appeal within the context of the assigned grade.

Proof
1938

MINTAGE
8,152

RARITY RANKINGS

Overall, All Proof Grades: 3rd of 7
High Grade, Proof-65 or Finer: 3rd of 7

Important Varieties: None.

General Comments: The proofs in the Walking Liberty Half Dollar series have relative rarity rankings that are comparable to their original mintages. The 1938 has the third-lowest mintage in this series, and it is also the third-rarest issue after the 1936 and 1937. Most survivors are concentrated in the Proof-64 to Proof-66 grade range. Proof-67s are somewhat scarce, but enough are around that finding one should not prove all that difficult an endeavor. Proof-68s, on the other hand, are very rare.

Strike: This is a very well-made issue, and the typical example has full striking detail. Every once in a while, however, a proof 1938 is encountered on which the highest elements of Liberty's right (facing) hand on the obverse and/or the inside of the eagle's trailing leg feathers on the reverse will be just a tad softly impressed.

Finish: The typical proof 1938 has an all-brilliant finish with uniform reflectivity over the devices and in the fields. There are, however, more examples of this issue with appreciable field-to-device contrast than there are for the proof 1936 or the proof 1937. PCGS and NGC have even bestowed a Cameo designation on four proof 1938 Half Dollars (December/2007).

Surfaces: When present at all, hairlines on a proof 1938 Half Dollar are usually few in number and seldom overly distracting. There are many examples that grade Proof-66 and finer on which hairlines and other signs of mishandling are so minor as to be virtually nonexistent.

Toning: The majority of proof 1938 Half Dollars that I have encountered are either untoned with bright, silver-white surfaces or lightly toned in hazy silver-gray or golden-tan patina. Coins with vivid red, blue and/or gold colors at the rims exist in fewer numbers than they do for the proof 1936 and proof 1937.

Eye Appeal: Eye appeal for this issue is almost always very good, if not excellent.

Significant Examples:

- **NGC Proof-66 Cameo.** *Ex: Atlanta, GA ANA Signature Auction (Heritage, 4/2006), lot 802, where it realized $4,313; Long Beach, CA Signature Coin Auction (Heritage, 2/2007), lot 4062, where it realized $4,083.*
- **NGC Proof-66 Cameo.** *Ex: Long Beach Signature Sale (Heritage, 9/2004), lot 6871, where it realized $7,475.*
- **NGC Proof-68.** *Ex: Baltimore Auction (Bowers and Merena, 11/2006), lot 3391, where it realized $3,795.*
- **PCGS Proof-68.** *Ex: Baltimore Auction (Bowers and Merena, 3/2006), lot 1486, where it realized $7,475.*
- **PCGS Proof-68.** *Ex: Robert Moreno Collection (Heritage, 7/2005), lot 10072, where it realized $23,000.*
- **PCGS Proof-68.** *Ex: Frog Run Farm Collection (American Numismatic Rarities, 11/2004), lot 1426, where it realized $5,520.*

Total Known: 2,250-2,575 Coins

TOTAL KNOWN BY GRADE			
Proof-60 to Proof-63	**Proof-64**	**Proof-65**	**Proof-66 or Finer**
185-235 Coins	525-575 Coins	650-750 Coins	900-1,000 Coins

VALUES BY GRADE			
Proof-60	**Proof-63**	**Proof-65**	**Proof-67**
$350-$400	$475-$575	$750-$1,000	$1,500-$2,250

COLLECTING AND INVESTING STRATEGIES

Ever since the third-party grading services starting designating certain proof coins with Cameo and Deep/Ultra Cameo finishes, such pieces have become so popular that they are commanding significant premiums among both collectors and investors. So few proof 1938 Half Dollars have received a Cameo designation from PCGS and NGC, however, that it would be unrealistic for me to advise that you wait until one of those coins becomes available for purchase.

There are, however, many proof 1938 Half Dollars in regular (as opposed to Cameo-designated) holders that still display a significant amount of mint frost over the central devices. Such pieces are offered frequently enough that you should be able to acquire one within the space of a year to a year-and-a-half. These coins often trade for a premium even though they do not include a Cameo designation as part of the grade, particularly when the surfaces are free of hazy toning that could prevent full appreciation of modest field-to-device contrast.

1938

MINTAGE
4,110,000

RARITY RANKINGS

***Overall, Mint State:** 36th of 65 (Tie)*
***High Grade, MS-65 or Finer:** 39th of 65*

MIDDLE-DATE ISSUES
(1934-1940)

***Overall, Mint State:** 10th of 19 (Tie)*
***High Grade, MS-65 or Finer:** 13th of 19*

Important Varieties: None.

General Comments: An underrated issue, the 1938 is the rarest Philadelphia Mint Half Dollar struck from 1934 through 1940. Similar in overall rarity to the 1939-S, the 1938 is also more difficult to locate than the 1939-D and 1940-S in most Mint State grades. (Due to a poorer quality of strike, however, the 1940-S is a bit rarer in grades above MS-64.) Nevertheless, enough coins have survived that you should have little difficulty locating a 1938 in grades up to and including MS-65. MS-66s are scarce from a market availability standpoint, and a Superb Gem is a legitimately rare coin.

Strike: The 1938 typically comes with an overall, if not completely sharp strike. Lack of detail, when present at all, is usually minor and confined to the central obverse over and around Liberty's right (facing) hand.

Luster: Bright, frosty luster characterizes virtually all Mint State 1938 Half Dollars that I have seen.

Surfaces: Mint State examples range from lightly abraded to virtually pristine. The typical piece is minimally abraded with overall smooth-looking surfaces.

Toning: The 1938 is seldom encountered with more than light, iridescent toning, and most examples are fully brilliant with a frosty-white appearance.

Eye Appeal: Eye appeal is strong for this issue, and there are many attractive examples among the Mint State survivors.

Significant Examples:

- **PCGS MS-67.** *Ex: Milwaukee, WI ANA Signature Coin Auction (Heritage, 8/2007), lot 1099, where it realized $2,875.*
- **NGC MS-67.** *Ex: Milwaukee, WI ANA Signature Coin Auction (Heritage, 8/2007), lot 1100, where it realized $1,955.*
- **NGC MS-67.** *Ex: Vanek Collection (Heritage, 7/2007), lot 1055, where it realized $2,013.*
- **PCGS MS-67.** *Ex: Baltimore Auction (Bowers and Merena, 3/2006), lot 1487, where it realized $4,025.*
- **PCGS MS-67.** *Ex: Collections of Craig N. Smith and George William Youngman (Bowers and Merena, 3/2003), lot 1737, where it realized $3,163.*
- **PCGS MS-67.** *Ex: Rarities Sale (Bowers and Merena, 1/2003), lot 380, where it realized $4,370.*

Total Known in Mint State: 3,500-4,050 Coins

TOTAL KNOWN BY GRADE			
MS-60 to MS-63	**MS-64**	**MS-65**	**MS-66 or Finer**
475-525 Coins	1,075-1,275 Coins	1,350-1,550 Coins	600-700 Coins

VALUES BY GRADE			
MS-60	**MS-63**	**MS-65**	**MS-67**
$50-$75	$100-$150	$375-$425	$2,000-$3,000

COLLECTING AND INVESTING STRATEGIES

The 1938 is a well-produced, generally well-preserved issue that can be a real delight to behold in the finer Mint State grades. I recommend purchasing an MS-65 or MS-66 with bright, frosty-white surfaces and a sharp strike. You should have little difficulty finding such a coin in the numismatic market, but expect to pay a premium over what you would pay for, say a 1936 or 1937 in those grades because the 1938 has an appreciably smaller population. On the other hand, MS-65s and MS-66s are much more affordable than MS-67s. In fact, you will be saving approximately $1,450-$2,400 without sacrificing too much on technical quality or eye appeal by purchasing an MS-66 over an MS-67.

1938-D

MINTAGE
491,600

RARITY RANKINGS

Overall, Mint State: 32nd of 65
High Grade, MS-65 or Finer: 33rd of 65

MIDDLE-DATE ISSUES
(1934-1940)

Overall, Mint State: 7th of 19
High Grade, MS-65 or Finer: 7th of 19

Important Varieties: None.

General Comments: The 1938-D has the lowest mintage of any Walking Liberty Half Dollar struck from 1923 through 1947. Unlike the early-date Walking Liberty Half Dollars from 1916 through 1933, the 1938-D was saved in fairly significant numbers at the time of issue by dealers and collectors who believed that the low mintage would translate into strong numismatic demand in the coming decades. The speculators were correct, as the 1938-D has long commanded a significant premium even in the lowest *circulated* grades.

Owing to widespread hoarding on release of the issue, Mint State survivors are more plentiful than the mintage might suggest. The 1938-D still sells for more in Mint State than any other Walking Liberty Half Dollar struck from 1934 through 1947 because it has a smaller total population. It is also genuinely rarer in Mint State than the 1936-D, 1937-S, 1939-D, 1939-S and 1940-S, as well as all of the mintmarked issues produced from 1941-1947. The 1938-D, however, is overrated in Mint State when compared to the 1934-D, 1934-S, 1935-D, 1935-S, 1936-S and 1937-D. The typical Mint State 1938-D grades MS-60 to MS-65. MS-66s are moderately scarce, while a Superb Gem is a conditionally rare coin.

Strike: 1938-D Half Dollars are a bit softly struck over Liberty's right (facing) hand on the obverse and along the inside of the eagle's trailing leg on the reverse. A small number of coins display softness in the detail over the highpoints of Liberty's head or the eagle's breast. Far from the worst-struck issue in this series, even a softly impressed 1938-D offers a degree of separation between the thumb and index finger on Liberty's right (facing) hand.

Luster: Luster quality for this issue is very good, and it can be either satiny or softly frosted in finish.

Surfaces: Mint State 1938-D Half Dollars seldom have more than a few scattered abrasions. Despite the premium that this issue commands, it is actually not all that difficult to locate an overall smooth example that grades MS-65 or MS-66.

Toning: The typical example is fully brilliant with bright-white surfaces. If present, toning is generally light in color with an iridescent quality that does not inhibit the luster.

Eye Appeal: Despite the prevalence of minor striking incompleteness among surviving examples, the 1938-D has above-average eye appeal.

Significant Examples:

- **NGC MS-67.** *Ex: ANA Charlotte National Money Show Auction (Heritage, 3/2007), lot 1087, where it realized $4,313.*
- **NGC MS-67.** *Ex: Long Beach, CA Signature Coin Auction (Heritage, 9/2007), lot 1758, where it realized $4,169.*
- **PCGS MS-67.** *Ex: Denver, CO Signature & Platinum Night Auction (Heritage, 8/2006), lot 3520, where it realized $10,925.*
- **PCGS MS-67.** *Ex: Anne Kate Collection (Bowers and Merena, 11/2006), lot 3394, where it realized $7,188.*
- **PCGS MS-67.** *Ex: Kallenberg Registry Set of Walking Liberty Half Dollars 1933 to 1947 (Heritage, 11/2005), lot 2713, where it realized $6,325.*
- **PCGS MS-67.** *Ex: Pittsburgh Rarities Sale (Bowers and Merena, 8/2004), lot 707; ANA National Money Show Auction (Bowers and Merena, 4/2006), lot 619, where it realized $16,675. The coin did not sell in the first-listed auction.*

Total Known in Mint State: 2,300-2,600 Coins

TOTAL KNOWN BY GRADE			
MS-60 to MS-63	**MS-64**	**MS-65**	**MS-66 or Finer**
350-400 Coins	775-875 Coins	850-950 Coins	325-375 Coins

VALUES BY GRADE			
MS-60	**MS-63**	**MS-65**	**MS-67**
$375-$475	$575-$675	$1,250-$1,500	$4,000-$8,000+

COLLECTING AND INVESTING STRATEGIES

Due to a limited mintage and strong demand, the 1938-D is an obvious choice for inclusion in an investment portfolio. I would stay away from coins that grade lower than MS-64 as these tend to have noticeably abraded surfaces and/or subdued luster. Also, toned examples on which the colors are hazy in appearance tend to trade at a discount and should be avoided. Look for bright, preferably brilliant coins with smooth-looking surfaces and at least bold definition over and around the central obverse highpoint. A well-struck MS-65 or MS-66 with frosty-white surfaces would make an impressive addition to any collection.

Proof
1939

MINTAGE
8,808

RARITY RANKINGS

Overall, All Proof Grades: *4th of 7*
High Grade, Proof-65 or Finer: *4th of 7*

Important Varieties: None.

General Comments: A bit more obtainable than the proof 1938, the proof 1939 is usually offered in grades that range from Proof-64 through Proof-67. Proof-68s are moderately rare, but enough are around that buying opportunities for such coins usually come along several times yearly.

Strike: The typical proof 1939 is fully struck over even the most intricate elements of the design. As with the proof 1938, however, there are a few examples of this issue that are a bit softly defined over Liberty's right (facing) hand in the center of the obverse and/or along the inside of the eagle's trailing leg on the reverse.

Finish: Like all proof Walking Liberty Half Dollars, the 1939 was produced using all-brilliant proofing techniques. While most examples are uniformly mirrored in finish, a significant number of coins are known with noticeable mint frost over the central devices. The frost, however, is seldom as thick as it is on the few proof 1938 Half Dollars that have this attribute. The major grading services have designated only two examples with a Cameo finish, both of which are at PCGS (December/2007).

Surfaces: Wispy hairlines are either minimal in number or virtually nonexistent.

Toning: While many examples are untoned, a considerable number of proof 1939 Half Dollars exhibit light-to-moderate toning with either iridescent or hazy qualities. The more attractively toned coins almost always exhibit golden-tan, ice-blue, sea-green and/or reddish-orange colors.

Eye Appeal: As an issue, the proof 1939 has strong eye appeal.

Significant Examples:

  • **NGC Proof-68.** *Ex: Summer FUN Signature Coin Auction (Heritage, 7/2007), lot 1107, where it realized $3,220.*

- **PCGS Proof-68.** *Ex: Long Beach Signature Auction (Heritage, 2/2006), lot 1547, where it realized $6,325.*
- **NGC Proof-68★.** *Ex: Rarities Sale (Bowers and Merena, 8/2004), lot 708, where it realized $4,600.*
- **NGC Proof-68★.** *Ex: New York Invitational Sale (David Lawrence, 7/2004), lot 3177, where it realized $5,060.*
- **PCGS Proof-68.** *Ex: Rarities Sale (Bowers and Merena, 1/2003), lot 381, where it realized $4,830.*
- **NGC Proof-68.** *Ex: California Sale (Ira & Larry Goldberg, 10/2000), lot 1738, where it realized $2,415.*

Total Known: 2,500-2,900 Coins

TOTAL KNOWN BY GRADE			
Proof-60 to Proof-63	Proof-64	Proof-65	Proof-66 or Finer
150-200 Coins	475-525 Coins	675-775 Coins	1,200-1,400 Coins

VALUES BY GRADE			
Proof-60	Proof-63	Proof-65	Proof-67
$300-$350	$425-$525	$700-$900	$925-$1,500

COLLECTING AND INVESTING STRATEGIES

Like the proof 1938, the proof 1939 is a particularly attractive coin when it includes a degree of contrast between the fields and the central devices. This feature is often less noticeable for the proof 1939 than it is for the proof 1938, and many examples only have light mint frost to Liberty's portrait on the obverse while the reverse eagle is essentially fully brilliant. Look for a coin with light mint frost on both of these devices, and then make sure that it is fully untoned so that the cameo-like contrast that is present is readily evident.

If you have a penchant for original toning, you could also do well with the proof 1939 by selecting a coin with ice-blue and/or reddish-orange colors. These are the most vivid shades that I have ever seen on a proof Half Dollar of this date. Chances are the toning will be somewhat mottled with the most extensive and/or vivid colors confined to the peripheries. This is a perfectly acceptable trait that is actually characteristic of the toning found on many proof Walking Liberty Half Dollars irrespective of date.

1939

MINTAGE
6,812,000

RARITY RANKINGS

Overall, Mint State: 44th of 65
High Grade, MS-65 or Finer: 49th of 65

MIDDLE-DATE ISSUES
(1934-1940)

Overall, Mint State: 18th of 19
High Grade, MS-65 or Finer: 19th of 19

Important Varieties: None.

General Comments: This is a plentiful issue that is readily obtainable in all grades through MS-66, although the 1939 has a slightly smaller Mint State population than the 1940. The 1939 also has the highest certified population in MS-67 of any Walking Liberty Half Dollar produced up to that point in time and can only be described as moderately scarce. MS-68s, on the other hand, are rare.

Strike: The 1939 is a well-struck issue and the typical example is sharply defined. You might have difficulty locating a fully struck coin, however, as most pieces that I have seen have a touch of softness to the highpoint detail in the center of the obverse.

Luster: The 1939 has excellent luster that is almost always fully frosted in texture.

Surfaces: Mint State coins run the gamut from noticeably abraded to virtually free of abrasions. The typical example is quite smooth with no more than two or three small abrasions.

Toning: There are many fully brilliant examples from which to choose in the market. Toned coins are seen less often, and these usually have light patina that is neither particularly vibrant nor especially attractive. The vivid Gem that I have selected as the plate coin at the beginning of this section is one of the most colorfully and attractively toned 1939 Half Dollars that I have ever seen.

Eye Appeal: The 1939 has above-average, if not strong eye appeal.

Significant Examples:

- **PCGS MS-68.** *Ex: James W. Lull Collection (Bowers and Merena, 1/2005), lot 701, where it realized $5,175; Baltimore Auction (Bowers and Merena, 11/2007), lot 2372. The coin did not sell in the latter auction.*
- **PCGS MS-68.** *Ex: Denver ANA Auction (Bowers and Merena, 8/2006), lot 3501, where it realized $9,488; Houston, TX U.S. Signature Coin Auction (Heritage, 11/2007), lot 61013, where it realized $7,475.*
- **NGC MS-68.** *Ex: Vanek Collection (Heritage, 7/2007), lot 1061, where it realized $4,169.*
- **PCGS MS-68.** *Ex: Kallenberg Registry Set of Walking Liberty Half Dollars 1933 to 1947 (Heritage, 11/2005), lot 2714, where it realized $6,325; Long Beach Signature Auction (Heritage, 2/2006), lot 1476, where it realized $9,200.*
- **NGC MS-68.** *Ex: New York Invitational Sale (David Lawrence, 7/2004), lot 3152, where it realized $3,105.*
- **NGC MS-68.** *Ex: "Elite" Sale (Superior, 1/2002), lot 1166, where it realized $1,955.*

Total Known in Mint State: 5,725-6,725+ Coins

TOTAL KNOWN BY GRADE			
MS-60 to MS-63	**MS-64**	**MS-65**	**MS-66 or Finer**
625-725+ Coins	1,400-1,600+ Coins	2,000-2,500 Coins	1,700-1,900 Coins

VALUES BY GRADE			
MS-60	**MS-63**	**MS-65**	**MS-67**
$30-$40	$55-$65	$150-$250	$475-$575

COLLECTING AND INVESTING STRATEGIES

Many collectors and investors choose to collect the later-date Walking Liberty Half Dollars with bright, brilliant surfaces. This is a particularly sound strategy as far as the 1939 is concerned. I am unimpressed with the toning that is usually found on Half Dollars of this issue. It is often of a dull silver-gray or golden-tan color with a splotchy distribution – both of which are attributes that can be distracting to the viewer. As previously stated, the plate coin at the beginning of this section is a noteworthy exception in that it possesses vivid, attractive toning.

1939-D

MINTAGE
4,267,800

**RARITY
RANKINGS**

Overall, Mint State: 42nd of 65
High Grade, MS-65 or Finer: 45th of 65

**MIDDLE-DATE ISSUES
(1934-1940)**
Overall, Mint State: 16th of 19
High Grade, MS-65 or Finer: 16th of 19

Important Varieties: There is an important variety for this issue, and it is a Repunched Mintmark with the attributions FS-501 and Fox V-101.

General Comments: The 1939-D is the most common mintmarked Walking Liberty Half Dollar produced from 1934-1940, edging out the 1940-S in terms of total number of Mint State coins known and the 1939-S in high grades. Examples are readily obtainable in all grades through MS-66. Superb Gems, however, exist in limited numbers. MS-67s are rare and MS-68s are all but unobtainable.

Strike: Striking quality for this issue is very similar to that of the 1938-D. Most examples have at least some degree of softness to the detail over Liberty's right (facing) hand and the inside of the eagle's trailing leg. Some coins are actually quite blunt in these areas. On the other hand, lack of detail to Liberty's head and the eagle's breast is usually minor, if present at all.

Luster: Bright, effulgent luster is the norm for this issue. Most examples that I have seen are frosty, but satiny coins are occasionally encountered in the market.

Surfaces: With a large population of Mint State survivors, it should come as no surprise to read that the 1939-D varies widely in terms of surface preservation. Most examples, however, are no more than lightly abraded, and smooth-looking coins are obtainable with minimal effort.

Toning: The typical 1939-D is either fully brilliant or lightly toned. Moderately-to-deeply toned examples are encountered only once in a while. Unlike the 1939, the 1939-D tends to be quite attractive when toning is present on one or both sides.

Eye Appeal: This issue has above-average eye appeal, and coins with relatively bold striking detail in the center of the obverse are almost always highly attractive.

Significant Examples:

• **NGC MS-68★.** *Ex: ANA Charlotte National Money Show Auction (Heritage, 3/2007), lot 1092, where it realized $6,325.*

• **NGC MS-68.** *Ex: ANA Charlotte National Money Show Auction (Heritage, 3/2007), lot 1093, where it realized $3,220.*

Total Known in Mint State: 5,100-5,700+ Coins

TOTAL KNOWN BY GRADE			
MS-60 to MS-63	**MS-64**	**MS-65**	**MS-66 or Finer**
450-500+ Coins	1,425-1,625 Coins	2,175-2,375 Coins	1,000-1,200 Coins

VALUES BY GRADE			
MS-60	**MS-63**	**MS-65**	**MS-67**
$35-$45	$60-$70	$150-$250	$925-$1,500

COLLECTING AND INVESTING STRATEGIES

Whether you choose to pursue a brilliant coin or a toned example, you should have little difficulty locating an attractive 1939-D with few, if any outwardly noticeable abrasions. Be sure, however, to avoid coins that are completely lacking in detail over and around Liberty (right) facing hand in the center of the obverse.

1939-S

MINTAGE
2,552,000

RARITY RANKINGS

Overall, Mint State: 36th of 65 (Tie)
High Grade, MS-65 or Finer: 41st of 65

MIDDLE-DATE ISSUES
(1934-1940)

Overall, Mint State: 10th of 19 (Tie)
High Grade, MS-65 or Finer: 15th of 19

Important Varieties: None.

General Comments: The 1939-S has a smaller Mint State population than the 1939-D and 1940-S, but it is better produced than the 1940-S and, hence, easier to obtain in high grades. Coins that grade MS-60 to MS-66 should prove relatively easy to obtain. MS-67s, on the other hand, are scarce, and the 1939-S is unknown any finer.

Strike: Striking quality for this issue varies from overall sharp to noticeably soft. The typical example will have at least some lack of detail over and around Liberty's right (facing) hand in the center of the obverse, and many coins are actually quite blunt in that area. The reverse, however, seldom exhibits noteworthy lack of definition.

Luster: This is a highly lustrous issue, and most examples have a thick, rich, frosty texture to the surfaces.

Surfaces: The 1939-S is seldom encountered with more than a few scattered abrasions, and many examples are quite smooth with no noteworthy distractions.

Toning: Much more so than either the 1939 or 1939-D, the 1939-S ranges from brilliant to moderately toned. The toned coins typically have softer colors in silver, gold, tan and/or pinkish-rose shades.

Eye Appeal: Eye appeal is very good, if not excellent for both toned coins and brilliant examples.

Significant Examples:

- **PCGS MS-67.** *Ex: CSNS Signature Coin Auction (Heritage, 5/2007), lot 3037, where it realized $1,094.*
- **PCGS MS-67.** *Ex: ANA Charlotte National Money Show Auction (Heritage, 3/2007), lot 1094, where it realized $1,380.*
- **NGC MS-67.** *Ex: New York Invitational Sale (David Lawrence, 7/2004), lot 3154, where it realized $1,380.*
- **PCGS MS-67.** *Ex: Anne Kate Collection (Bowers and Merena, 11/2006), lot 3408, where it realized $3,048.*
- **PCGS MS-67.** *Ex: Baltimore Auction (Bowers and Merena, 7/2006), lot 1153, where it realized $2,185.*
- **NGC MS-67.** *Ex: Classics Sale (American Numismatic Rarities, 1/2004), lot 1509, where it realized $1,380.*

Total Known in Mint State: 3,500-4,050 Coins

TOTAL KNOWN BY GRADE			
MS-60 to MS-63	**MS-64**	**MS-65**	**MS-66 or Finer**
200-250 Coins	675-775 Coins	1,475-1,675 Coins	1,150-1,350 Coins

VALUES BY GRADE			
MS-60	**MS-63**	**MS-65**	**MS-67**
$100-$125	$140-$160	$250-$400	$1,050-$1,500

COLLECTING AND INVESTING STRATEGIES

Although elusive, sharply struck 1939-S Walking Liberty Half Dollars do exist and are numbered among the finer examples of the issue. It is a good idea to hold out until such a coin becomes available. While reality dictates that your set will have to obtain more-or-less softly struck examples of many issues in this series, the 1939-S should not be among them.

Proof
1940

MINTAGE
11,279

RARITY RANKINGS

Overall, All Proof Grades: 5th of 7
High Grade, Proof-65 or Finer: 5th of 7

Important Varieties: None.

General Comments: The 1940 is the first proof Walking Liberty Half Dollar with a mintage of more than 10,000 coins. It is more common than the four proof issues from 1936-1939. You should have no difficulty finding an example that grades Proof-64 through Proof-67, as this is the range in which most survivors are concentrated. Proof-68s are rare, yet obtainable with patience.

Strike: The strike for this issue is almost always full. Incompleteness of detail, when present, is never more than minor in nature and usually confined to the highest point in the center of the obverse and/or the inside of the eagle's trailing leg on the reverse.

Finish: Examples of this issue range in finish from brilliant throughout to very lightly frosted over the central devices. Neither PCGS nor NGC has certified a single example with a Cameo finish (December/2007).

Surfaces: A carefully preserved issue, the typical proof 1940 is either overall smooth or virtually pristine. Even those examples that do possess noticeable hairlines here and there are still usually free of distracting blemishes in most areas.

Toning: Proof 1940 Half Dollars are found both brilliant and lightly toned. The toned coins tend to have somewhat hazy colors in golden-tan, silver-gray and/or ice-blue. I have seen a few particularly attractive specimens with vivid red, orange and/or emerald-green toning that, when present, is usually confined to the peripheries.

Eye Appeal: The eye appeal for this issue is nothing less than strong.

Significant Examples:

- **PCGS Proof-68.** *Ex: Baltimore Auction (Bowers and Merena, 3/2006), lot 1491, where it realized $2,542.*

• **NGC Proof-68★.** *Ex: FUN Signature Coin Auction (Heritage, 1/2006), lot 4143, where it realized $3,450.*

• **PCGS Proof-68.** *Ex: Robert Moreno Collection (Heritage, 7/2005), lot 10074, where it realized $6,325.*

• **NGC Proof-68.** *Ex: Rarities Sale (Bowers and Merena, 5/2004), lot 244, where it realized $5,175.*

• **NGC Proof-68.** *Ex: Pre-Long Beach Elite Coin Auction (Superior, 5/2003), lot 2672, where it realized $2,530.*

• **NGC Proof-68.** *Ex: Pre-Long Beach Elite Coin Auction (Superior, 5/2003), lot 2673, where it realized $3,220.*

Total Known: 3,000-3,350 Coins

TOTAL KNOWN BY GRADE			
Proof-60 to Proof-63	Proof-64	Proof-65	Proof-66 or Finer
200-250 Coins	575-675 Coins	900-1,000 Coins	1,250-1,450 Coins

VALUES BY GRADE			
Proof-60	Proof-63	Proof-65	Proof-67
$275-$325	$350-$450	$550-$850	$800-$1,250

COLLECTING AND INVESTING STRATEGIES

As with the other proof issues in the Walking Liberty Half Dollar series, it is best to avoid any example of the 1940 with overly hazy toning that obscures the underlying mint brilliance.

1940

MINTAGE
9,156,000

RARITY
RANKINGS

Overall, Mint State: 45th of 65
High Grade, MS-65 or Finer: 48th of 65

MIDDLE-DATE ISSUES
(1934-1940)

Overall, Mint State: 19th of 19
High Grade, MS-65 or Finer: 18th of 19

Important Varieties: None.

General Comments: After only the 1936, the 1940 is the most common Philadelphia Mint delivery among the middle-date issues in the Walking Liberty Half Dollar series. Examples are readily obtainable in all grades through Superb Gem Mint State, although MS-67s are moderately scarce. A small number of MS-68s are known, and there is even a single MS-69 at NGC (December/2007).

Strike: The 1940 is a generally well-struck issue. Most examples have sharp definition. This is a high-mintage issue, however, and there are also many coins known that have noticeable softness of strike at Liberty's head and right (facing) hand on the obverse. The reverse tends to be better struck even on the more poorly produced examples, but slight lack of detail is sometimes seen on a few of the eagle's breast and trailing leg feathers.

Luster: The 1940 has excellent luster that is almost always fully frosted in texture. A few satiny examples are known, but these are in the minority among Mint State survivors.

Surfaces: Mint State examples run the gamut from noticeably abraded to virtually perfect. The typical 1940, however, is well preserved with few, if any, individually distracting abrasions.

Toning: Brilliant surfaces are the norm for this issue, and those examples that are toned tend to have only light, iridescent overtones.

Eye Appeal: The 1940 almost always has strong eye appeal, but lower-grade and/or lightly struck Mint State examples tend to be closer to average in this regard.

Significant Examples:

  • **PCGS MS-68.** *Ex: Summer FUN Signature Coin Auction (Heritage, 7/2007), lot 1064, where it realized $8,050.*

  • **PCGS MS-68.** *Ex: Anne Kate Collection (Bowers and Merena, 11/2006), lot 3413, where it realized $6,095.*

  • **PCGS MS-68.** *Ex: Denver ANA Auction (Bowers and Merena, 8/2006), lot 3510, where it realized $5,060.*

  • **NGC MS-68.** *Ex: Pre-Long Beach Elite Coin Auction (Superior, 5/2003), lot 2676, where it realized $5,463; FUN Signature Coin Auction (Heritage, 1/2007), lot 4789, where it realized $3,335.*

  • **PCGS MS-68.** *Ex: Pre-Long Beach Elite Coin Auction (Superior, 5/2003), lot 2675, where it realized $5,463.*

  • **PCGS MS-68.** *Ex: "Elite" Sale (Superior, 1/2002), lot 1167, where it realized $2,070.*

Total Known in Mint State: 6,200-7,000+ Coins

TOTAL KNOWN BY GRADE			
MS-60 to MS-63	**MS-64**	**MS-65**	**MS-66 or Finer**
800-900+ Coins	1,600-1,800+ Coins	2,250-2,500 Coins	1,550-1,750 Coins

VALUES BY GRADE			
MS-60	**MS-63**	**MS-65**	**MS-67**
$20-$30	$40-$60	$150-$250	$450-$850

COLLECTING AND INVESTING STRATEGIES

This is one of several issues in the Walking Liberty Half Dollar series for which you can afford to be highly selective. Do not accept any coin with bothersome lack of detail or noticeable abrasions, particularly those that are sizeable and/or located in prime focal areas. I prefer fully brilliant, frosty-white coins but, if you want to acquire a toned example, make sure that it is neither hazy nor splotchy in appearance.

1940-S

MINTAGE
4,550,000

**RARITY
RANKINGS**

Overall, Mint State: 41st of 65
High Grade, MS-65 or Finer: 38th of 65

**MIDDLE-DATE ISSUES
(1934-1940)**

Overall, Mint State: 15th of 19
High Grade, MS-65 or Finer: 12th of 19

Important Varieties: None.

General Comments: The 1940-S is the only mintmarked Half Dollar of the year. With a sizeable mintage and a good rate of survival, the 1940-S is easily obtainable in all grades through MS-65. Deficiencies with the strike, however, cause the certified population to dwindle rapidly beginning at the MS-66 grade level. Superb Gems are exceedingly rare and probably number no more than eight-to-ten coins. Among the middle-date issues in this series, the 1940-S is rarer than the 1939-D and 1939-S in high grades.

Strike: Beginning with this issue, significant striking problems return to plague the Walking Liberty Half Dollars struck in the San Francisco Mint. Expect the typical 1940-S to be softly struck with blunt definition over and around Liberty's head, right (facing) hand, the eagle's breast and right (facing) shoulder and/or the inside of the trailing leg feathers. Even a coin with the slightest degree of separation between the thumb and index finger on the right (facing) hand possesses an above-average strike by the standards of this issue.

Luster: Whereas strike is a noteworthy problem for the 1940-S, luster quality is a strong suit. Most Mint State examples possess vibrant, fully frosted luster. Satiny coins are not seen all that often.

Surfaces: It is lack of highpoint definition, rather than excessive abrasions, that prevent many 1940-S Half Dollars from grading higher than MS-65. The typical example is only lightly abraded, at best, and many examples are quite smooth.

Toning: Every once in a while, a 1940-S Half Dollar with light, iridescent toning appears in the market, and those coins tend to be very attractive with colorful highlights either at the rims or throughout. Most examples, nonetheless, are fully brilliant.

Eye Appeal: Due to the aforementioned deficiencies with the strike, the 1940-S has only average eye appeal.

Significant Examples:

• **NGC MS-67.** *Ex: Dallas, TX U.S. Coin Signature Auction (Heritage, 11/2007), lot 875, where it realized $5,175.*

• **NGC MS-67.** *Ex: Summer FUN Signature Sale (Heritage, 7/2007), lot 1070, where it realized $4,025.*

• **NGC MS-67.** *Ex: Robert Moreno Collection (Heritage, 7/2005), lot 10046, where it realized $13,800; ANA Charlotte National Money Show Auction (Heritage, 3/2007), lot 1100, where it realized $2,990.*

• **PCGS MS-67.** *Ex: Anne Kate Collection (Bowers and Merena, 11/2006), lot 3415, where it realized $32,775.*

• **NGC MS-67.** *Ex: Long Beach, CA Signature Coin Auction (Heritage, 9/2006), lot 2189; Dallas Signature Coin Auction (Heritage, 11/2006), lot 980, where it realized $7,475.*

Total Known in Mint State: 5,025-5,900+ Coins

TOTAL KNOWN BY GRADE			
MS-60 to MS-63	**MS-64**	**MS-65**	**MS-66 or Finer**
975-1,100+ Coins	2,200-2,700 Coins	1,500-1,700 Coins	350-400 Coins

VALUES BY GRADE			
MS-60	**MS-63**	**MS-65**	**MS-67**
$40-$50	$50-$65	$250-$350	$3,000-$8,000+

COLLECTING AND INVESTING STRATEGIES

The 1940-S is a leading strike rarity in the Walking Liberty Half Dollar series. In order to make sure that you are purchasing a coin that will catch the eye of future buyers and, hence, bring a strong sale price, you must insist on above-average striking detail. Most such examples are concentrated at the MS-66 and MS-67 grade levels. Superb Gems are extremely rare and quite costly, but a nice MS-66 can be had for between $750 and $900. Try to find an MS-66 with at least some separation between the thumb and index finger on Liberty's right (facing) hand. There are even a few examples with relatively bold definition in the centers. Do not, however, hold out for a coin with 100% full striking definition – I have never seen one and doubt that the 1940-S exists with that kind of strike.

Proof
1941

MINTAGE
15,412

RARITY
RANKINGS

Overall, All Proof Grades: 6th of 7
High Grade, Proof-65 or Finer: 6th of 7

Important Varieties: Several examples are known on which the designer's monogram AW has been removed by excessive die polishing. This variety is attributed as Breen-5182 and Fox P-101.

General Comments: The 1941 is the most common issue in the proof Walking Liberty Half Dollar series after the 1942. This issue is readily obtainable through the Proof-67 grade level. Even Proof-68s, while rare in an absolute sense, trade frequently enough that your only impediment to acquiring one should be the cost.

Strike: The proof 1941 has superior striking quality to the proof 1938, proof 1939 and proof 1940. Virtually all examples that I have seen are fully struck, and there seems to be fewer coins with trivial softness to the highpoint definition than there are for the 1938-1940 proof issues.

Finish: Typically offered with an all-brilliant finish, the proof 1941 occasionally has a bit of light mint frost to the central devices. I have never seen an example with enough field-to-device contrast to qualify for a Cameo designation from PCGS or NGC.

Surfaces: The vast majority of proof 1941 Half Dollars that have survived are either overall smooth or essentially pristine.

Toning: Examples range from fully brilliant to moderately toned. Toning for this issue tends to be a bit hazy, and it is often of a silver-gray or golden-tan color. Coins with vivid red, orange and blue highlights do exist, but they can be difficult to locate.

Eye Appeal: With the exception of those coins that are toned in overly hazy and/or mottled colors that subdue the underlying mint brilliance, the proof 1941 has strong eye appeal.

Significant Examples:

• **NGC Proof-68.** *Ex: Anaheim Auction (Bowers and Merena, 5/2006), lot 1163, where it realized $2,990.*

• **NGC Proof-68.** *Ex: CSNS Signature Auction (Heritage, 5/2005) lot 7538. This coin is an example of the No "AW" (Breen-5182) variety, and it did not sell in that auction.*

• **PCGS Proof-68.** *Ex: Bruce Scher #1 All-Time PCGS Registry Set (Heritage, 2/2005), lot 4137, where it realized $7,475.*

• **NGC Proof-68.** *Ex: New York Invitational (David Lawrence, 7/2004), lot 3179, where it realized $4,370.*

• **PCGS Proof-68.** *Ex: Pre-Long Beach Sale (Ira & Larry Goldberg, 1/2004), lot 2470, where it realized $4,888.*

• **NGC Proof-68.** *Ex: Pre-Long Beach Sale (Superior, 10/2000), lot 3473, where it realized $1,322.*

Total Known: 3,900-4,500 Coins

TOTAL KNOWN BY GRADE			
Proof-60 to Proof-63	**Proof-64**	**Proof-65**	**Proof-66 or Finer**
275-325 Coins	900-1,000 Coins	1,250-1,450 Coins	1,500-1,700 Coins

VALUES BY GRADE			
Proof-60	**Proof-63**	**Proof-65**	**Proof-67**
$225-$275	$375-$475	$525-$750	$800-$1,200

COLLECTING AND INVESTING STRATEGIES

There are no pointers that I can provide for this issue other than to avoid any coin with overly hazy toning and subdued brilliance.

1941

MINTAGE
24,192,000

RARITY
RANKINGS

Overall, Mint State: 61st of 65
High Grade, MS-65 or Finer: 62nd of 65

LATE-DATE ISSUES
(1941-1947)

Overall, Mint State: 16th of 20
High Grade, MS-65 or Finer: 17th of 20

Important Varieties: None.

General Comments: The 1941 is one of the most common issues in the entire Walking Liberty Half Dollar series, and it is readily obtainable in all grades from MS-60 to MS-66. This issue, however, is not quite as plentiful as the 1942, 1943, 1945 or 1946-D. Superb Gems are relatively common by the standards of this series, but few 1941 Half Dollars grade finer than MS-67.

Strike: The 1941 was produced in large numbers to help fuel the United States' expanding economy in the year leading up to the Japanese attack on Pearl Harbor. Perhaps not surprisingly, striking quality varies among the survivors, although it is seldom excessively soft. The typical example is actually quite sharp with little, if any lack of detail over isolated highpoints of the design.

Luster: The 1941 almost always comes with strong luster. Most examples have a frosty texture to the surfaces.

Surfaces: This is definitely one of the easier Walking Liberty Half Dollars to locate with overall smooth or virtually pristine surfaces.

Toning: The vast majority of survivors are fully brilliant and frosty-white in sheen. Occasionally, you will encounter a lightly toned example with delicate iridescent overtones. The few moderately toned examples that I have seen are almost all highly attractive with vivid colors.

Eye Appeal: The typical 1941 has strong eye appeal.

Significant Examples:

- **NGC MS-68.** *Ex: ANA Charlotte National Money Show Auction (Heritage, 3/2007), lot 1101, where it realized $1,495.*
- **PCGS MS-68.** *Ex: Anne Kate Collection (Bowers and Merena, 11/2006), lot 3418, where it realized $6,325.*
- **NGC MS-68.** *Ex: Dallas Signature Coin Auction (Heritage, 10/2006), lot 2121, where it realized $2,530.*
- **NGC MS-68★.** *Ex: FUN Signature Coin Auction (Heritage, 1/2006), lot 4088, where it realized $3,680. This is one of the most vividly toned 1941 Half Dollars that I have ever encountered.*
- **PCGS MS-68.** *Ex: Palm Bach, FL Signature Sale (Heritage, 11/2004), lot 7007, where it realized $5,290.*
- **PCGS MS-68.** *Ex: Long Beach Signature Sale (Heritage, 2/2003), lot 7004, where it realized $6,325.*

Total Known in Mint State: 15,250-17,500+ Coins

TOTAL KNOWN BY GRADE			
MS-60 to MS-63	MS-64	MS-65	MS-66 or Finer
1,750-1,950+ Coins	3,775-4,225+ Coins	5,625-6,625 Coins	4,100-4,600 Coins

VALUES BY GRADE			
MS-60	MS-63	MS-65	MS-67
$25-$30	$35-$40	$120-$150	$400-$600

COLLECTING AND INVESTING STRATEGIES

For a common Walking Liberty Half Dollar such as this, you would be best served by emphasizing eye appeal over investment potential when the time comes to buy. Rest assured that if you select a high-grade, attractive coin with a sharp strike and no singularly distracting abrasions, you will also be doing all within your power to guarantee a strong return on your investment in an example of this issue.

1941-D

MINTAGE
11,248,400

**RARITY
RANKINGS**

Overall, Mint State: 50th of 65
High Grade, MS-65 or Finer: 55th of 65

**LATE-DATE ISSUES
(1941-1947)**
Overall, Mint State: 5th of 20
High Grade, MS-65 or Finer: 11th of 20

Important Varieties: There is a prominent Repunched Mintmark variety attributed as FS-501 and Fox V-101.

General Comments: The 1941-D is the third-rarest Denver Mint issue in the late-date Walking Liberty Half Dollar series after the 1942-D and 1943-D. In an absolute sense, however, this is one of the most common Denver Mint Half Dollars of this type. Examples are readily obtainable in all grades up to and including MS-66. MS-67s are scarce, but enough exist that you should have little difficulty acquiring one given enough time and financial resources. Coins that grade any finer, however, are all but unknown.

Strike: As an issue, the 1941-D is not quite as well struck as the 1941, and a greater percentage of the survivors have noticeable lack of detail. This is particularly evident in and around the centers, where Liberty's right (facing) hand and the inside of the eagle's trailing leg often display varying degrees of softness to the strike. There are, however, enough sharply struck examples known that Cherrypicking will pay dividends.

Luster: The 1941-D has excellent luster that can be either satiny or frosty in texture. The frosty examples are particularly vibrant.

Surfaces: While many examples have noticeably abraded surfaces, the 1941-D has such a large population in the finer Mint State grades that it is an easy issue to locate with smooth, if not virtually pristine surfaces.

Toning: The coins that I have seen range from brilliant to moderately toned in appearance. Most of the toned coins have only light, iridescent overtones. It is not often that you will encounter a piece with deeper and/or more vivid colors.

Eye Appeal: Overall eye appeal for this issue is above average-to-strong.

Significant Examples: PCGS and NGC have certified three examples of the 1941-D in MS-68 (December/2007). I am not aware of any auction sales for these coins during the eight-year period from 2000-2007.

Total Known in Mint State: 9,100-9,800+ Coins

TOTAL KNOWN BY GRADE			
MS-60 to MS-63	MS-64	MS-65	MS-66 or Finer
875-975+ Coins	2,325-2,525 Coins	3,900-4,100 Coins	2,000-2,200 Coins

VALUES BY GRADE			
MS-60	MS-63	MS-65	MS-67
$30-$35	$40-$45	$125-$175	$550-$1,100

COLLECTING AND INVESTING STRATEGIES

Paying attention to striking detail is the best way to maximize your investment potential in a 1941-D Walking Liberty Half Dollar. Acquire a coin with sharp definition that extends even to the central obverse highpoint and the inside of the eagle's trailing leg on the reverse. You may have to sift through a considerable number of average strikes in order to find a coin that meets this criterion, but rest assured that such examples do exist. In fact, a sharply struck 1941-D is really not a rare coin, and you should have several buying opportunities in any given year of numismatic trading.

1941-S

MINTAGE
8,098,000

RARITY RANKINGS

Overall, Mint State: 51st of 65
High Grade, MS-65 or Finer: 42nd of 65

LATE-DATE ISSUES
(1941-1947)

Overall, Mint State: 6th of 20
High Grade, MS-65 or Finer: 1st of 20

Important Varieties: A Repunched Mintmark variety is known: FS-501 and Fox V-102. This RPM has been mistakenly described as an S/Horizontal S in some numismatic references.

General Comments: Although long regarded as the rarest issue in the late-date Walking Liberty Half Dollar series, I believe that the 1941-S only deserves this title at or above the MS-65 grade level. This is really not a difficult issue to locate in grades through MS-64, and the 1941-S actually has a larger total Mint State population than the 1941-D (barely), 1942-D, 1942-S, 1943-D and 1943-S. Even MS-65s and MS-66s can be had without undue hardship, this despite the fact that the 1941-S is a noteworthy strike rarity. As a Superb Gem, however, the 1941-S is a genuinely rare coin.

Strike: The central obverse over and around Liberty's right (facing) hand is almost always softly defined on the 1941-S, as is the inside of the eagle's trailing leg on the reverse. Striking incompleteness for this issue can also touch Liberty's head and the eagle's breast and right (facing) shoulder. Many examples are unevenly struck with softness in one or more of these areas but relatively sharp detail over the balance of the devices. In 10 years as a professional numismatist I cannot recall seeing more than a handful of coins that were overall sharply struck. I have never seen a 1941-S with 100% full striking detail and doubt that such a coin exists.

Luster: Luster is generally vibrant with a satin or frosty sheen.

Surfaces: The 1941-S is one of the more challenging Half Dollars from the 1940s to locate without at least a few scattered abrasions.

Toning: Examples range from brilliant to moderately toned. The typical 1941-S, however, is either brilliant or lightly toned in iridescent shades.

Eye Appeal: The 1941-S has only average eye appeal, an assessment that I attribute primarily to deficiencies with the strike.

Significant Examples:

- **NGC MS-67.** *Ex: Long Beach, CA Signature Coin Auction (Heritage, 9/2007), lot 1768, where it realized $6,900.*
- **NGC MS-67.** *Ex: Long Beach, CA Signature Coin Auction (Heritage, 9/2007), lot 1769, where it realized $8,050.*
- **NGC MS-67.** *Ex: Long Beach Signature Auction (Heritage, 6/2006), lot 1881, where it realized $9,200; ANA Charlotte National Money Show Auction (Heritage, 3/2007), lot 1108, where it realized $8,625.*
- **PCGS MS-67.** *Ex: Anne Kate Collection (Bowers and Merena, 11/2006), lot 3423, where it realized $90,850.*
- **PCGS MS-67.** *Ex: San Francisco, CA ANA Signature Auction (Heritage, 7/2005), lot 10231, where it realized $20,300. This coin and the following example have two of the most complete strikes that I have ever seen on a 1941-S Half Dollar.*
- **PCGS MS-67.** *Ex: Ally Collection (Heritage, 7/2002), lot 8557, where it realized $13,800.*

Total Known in Mint State: 9,200-9,900 Coins

TOTAL KNOWN BY GRADE			
MS-60 to MS-63	**MS-64**	**MS-65**	**MS-66 or Finer**
2,200-2,400 Coins	4,225-4,425 Coins	2,100-2,300 Coins	675-775 Coins

VALUES BY GRADE			
MS-60	**MS-63**	**MS-65**	**MS-67**
$60-$70	$75-$115	$625-$1,000	$6,200-$20,000+

COLLECTING AND INVESTING STRATEGIES

If you are looking for only a few Walking Liberty Half Dollars to include in a diversified investment portfolio, I would skip the 1941-S. The issue is overpriced in relation to its actual rarity, and it can be difficult to find an attractive example due to incessant problems with the strike.

If you are assembling a partial or complete set of Walking Liberty Half Dollars, or if you must acquire a 1941-S for any other reason, try to find a coin with at least some separation between the thumb and index finger on Liberty's right (facing) hand. In addition, I suggest avoiding one of the moderately toned coins as the colors are seldom vivid or particularly attractive.

Proof
1942

MINTAGE
21,120

RARITY
RANKINGS

Overall, All Proof Grades: *7th of 7*
High Grade, Proof-65 or Finer: *7th of 7*

Important Varieties: None.

General Comments: The final issue in the proof Walking Liberty Half Dollar series, the 1942 is also the most plentiful. Examples are readily obtainable in all grades through Proof-67, and even Proof-68s are usually available for purchase several times yearly. The 1942 also has a larger certified population in Proof-69 than any other Half Dollar of this type, but such coins are still exceedingly rare when viewed in the wider context of the numismatic market.

Strike: The typical proof 1942 is very sharply, if not fully struck. Those coins that are not 100% full have only trivial lack of detail that is usually confined to the highest portion of Liberty's right (facing) hand on the obverse and the inside of the eagle's trailing leg on the reverse.

Finish: The majority of examples are fully brilliant in finish, although you will occasionally encounter a coin with light mint frost over the central devices. A proof 1942 with enough field-to-device contrast to secure a Cameo designation from PCGS or NGC is a very rare coin. In fact, both major grading services have assigned a Cameo designation to just five examples of this issue (December/2007).

Surfaces: This issue has been well cared for over the years, and the typical example is either overall smooth or virtually pristine. When present, signs of handling are usually small in size, few in number and not overly distracting.

Toning: There seems to be about a 50-50 mix of untoned coins and lightly-to-moderately toned examples in the market. The toned coins usually display either iridescent colors or hazy overtones. In both cases, the colors are typically gold, silver, powder-blue or tan and rarely a deeper shade such as red, orange or russet.

Eye Appeal: The proof 1942 usually has excellent eye appeal, although coins with hazy toning and subdued surfaces are seldom as attractive as brilliant or lightly toned pieces.

Significant Examples:

   • **NGC Proof-67 Cameo.** *Ex: Baltimore ANA Auction (Bowers and Merena, 7/2003), lot 1648, where it realized $3,450.*

   • **NGC Proof-69.** *Ex: Robert Moreno Collection (Heritage, 7/2005), lot 10076, where it realized $34,500.*

   • **PCGS Proof-69.** *Ex: Nicholas Collection (Heritage, 5/2004), lot 7857, where it realized $42,550; Bruce Scher #1 All-Time PCGS Registry Set (Heritage, 2/2005), lot 4138, where it realized $46,000.*

Total Known: 5,450-6,400 Coins

TOTAL KNOWN BY GRADE			
Proof-60 to Proof-63	**Proof-64**	**Proof-65**	**Proof-66 or Finer**
350-400 Coins	1,050-1,250 Coins	1,450-1,650 Coins	2,600-3,100 Coins

VALUES BY GRADE			
Proof-60	**Proof-63**	**Proof-65**	**Proof-67**
$225-$275	$375-$475	$500-$750	$800-$1,200

COLLECTING AND INVESTING STRATEGIES

There are no pointers that I can provide for this issue other than to avoid any coin with overly hazy toning and subdued brilliance.

1942

MINTAGE
47,818,000

**RARITY
RANKINGS**

Overall, Mint State: 64th of 65
High Grade, MS-65 or Finer: 63rd of 65

**LATE-DATE ISSUES
(1941-1947)**
Overall, Mint State: 19th of 20
High Grade, MS-65 or Finer: 18th of 20

Important Varieties: There is a prominent Doubled Die Reverse variety known for this issue, and it is attributed as FS-801 and Fox V-101.

General Comments: The 1942 is the most common Walking Liberty Half Dollar in Mint State after only the 1943, although it is also not quite as plentiful as the 1946-D in high grades. This issue is readily obtainable in all grades through MS-66. Superb Gems in MS-67 are moderately scarce, at best, but the 1942 is surprisingly elusive in MS-68. In fact, this issue is rarer in MS-68 than the lower-mintage 1939, 1940 and 1941.

Strike: As a high-mintage issue produced during the chaotic years of the Second World War, it should come as no surprise to read that striking quality for the 1942 varies considerably between examples. As a whole, however, the issue is well made, and most coins that I have seen are boldly, sharply or even fully struck. When present, lack of detail is seldom excessive and usually confined to Liberty's head, the central obverse over and around her right (facing) hand and/or the inside of the eagle's trailing leg.

Luster: The 1942 typically has very good, if not excellent luster that is either of a satin or frosty texture.

Surfaces: This is one of the easiest Walking Liberty Half Dollars to locate with carefully preserved surfaces.

Toning: Most Mint State examples are either brilliant or lightly toned in iridescent shades. With so many coins in the market, however, there are definitely exceptions to the norm.

Eye Appeal: Eye appeal for the 1942 is almost always excellent, and it is seldom less than very good except perhaps in the lowest Mint State grades where excessive abrasions and/or subdued luster can be a problem.

Significant Examples:

• **PCGS MS-68.** *Ex: ANA Charlotte National Money Show Auction (Heritage, 3/2007), lot 1110, where it realized $20,700.*

• **NGC MS-68.** *Ex: Dr. S. Long Collection; FUN Signature Sale (Heritage, 1/2005), lot 7795, where it realized $7,188; Palm Beach, FL Signature Auction (Heritage, 3/2006), lot 1566, where it realized $5,175; ANA Charlotte National Money Show Auction (Heritage, 3/2007), lot 1111, where it realized $2,530.*

Total Known in Mint State: 21,575-24,575+ Coins

TOTAL KNOWN BY GRADE			
MS-60 to MS-63	**MS-64**	**MS-65**	**MS-66 or Finer**
3,050-3,550+ Coins	7,000-8,000+ Coins	7,650-8,650 Coins	3,875-4,375 Coins

VALUES BY GRADE			
MS-60	**MS-63**	**MS-65**	**MS-67**
$25-$30	$35-$40	$100-$150	$475-$700

COLLECTING AND INVESTING STRATEGIES

For a common Walking Liberty Half Dollar such as this, you would be best served by emphasizing eye appeal over investment potential when the time comes to buy. Rest assured that if you select a high-grade, attractive coin with a sharp strike and no singularly distracting abrasions, you will also be doing all within your power to guarantee a strong return on your investment in an example of this issue.

1942-D

MINTAGE
10,973,800

**RARITY
RANKINGS**

Overall, Mint State: 46th of 65
High Grade, MS-65 or Finer: 50th of 65

**LATE-DATE ISSUES
(1941-1947)**
Overall, Mint State: 1st of 20
High Grade, MS-65 or Finer: 5th of 20

Important Varieties: None.

General Comments: The 1942-D was produced in large numbers for a Denver Mint issue in this series and is easy to obtain in the MS-60 to MS-66 grade range. The 1942-D, however, is actually the rarest late-date Walking Liberty Half Dollar in all Mint State grades. The number of survivors drops off precipitately above the MS-66 level. MS-67s are scarce and MS-68s are very rare.

Strike: The typical 1942-D is a bit softly struck over Liberty's right (facing) hand and the skirt lines over her left thigh. Incompleteness of detail is also seen quite often on Liberty's head and along the inside of the eagle's trailing leg, but these areas are usually better defined than the central obverse.

Luster: Luster is almost always very-good-to-excellent for this issue. I have seen both satiny and frosty coins, the latter much more frequently than the former.

Surfaces: Most 1942-D Half Dollars have a few more abrasions that the typical 1942, but enough coins are extant at the MS-65 and MS-66 grade levels that you should have little difficulty locating an overall smooth-looking example.

Toning: Brilliant or lightly toned surfaces are seen on the majority of Mint State 1942-D Half Dollars in the market. The toned coins typically have iridescent colors such as gold and silver, but peripherally toned examples tend to display slightly more vivid shades like orange, red, copper and/or russet.

Eye Appeal: The 1942-D has above-average, if not strong eye appeal.

Significant Examples:

• **NGC MS-68.** *Ex: Nevada Silver Collection; Houston, TX U.S. Signature Coin Auction (Heritage, 11/2007), lot 61014, where it realized $6,325.*

• **PCGS MS-68.** *Ex: Rarities Sale (Bowers and Merena, 1/2003), lot 385, where it realized $4,485.*

• **PCGS MS-68.** *Ex: Ally Collection (Heritage, 7/2002), lot 8559, where it realized $4,370.*

Total Known in Mint State: 7,150-8,150+ Coins

TOTAL KNOWN BY GRADE			
MS-60 to MS-63	**MS-64**	**MS-65**	**MS-66 or Finer**
725-825+ Coins	1,925-2,125 Coins	2,925-3,425 Coins	1,575-1,775 Coins

VALUES BY GRADE			
MS-60	**MS-63**	**MS-65**	**MS-67**
$25-$35	$45-$75	$150-$350	$700-$1,100

COLLECTING AND INVESTING STRATEGIES

The 1942-D was not saved to the same extent as the 1942. Most Mint State survivors show signs of below-average workmanship and careless handling in the Mint. Stick with coins that grade MS-65 or finer to avoid large and/or numerous abrasions, and try to find an example with above-average striking detail. Look for a minimum amount of softness to the definition in and around the central obverse, and avoid any 1942-D that is noticeably blunt over Liberty's right (facing) hand with little or no separation between the thumb and index finger.

1942-S

MINTAGE
12,708,000

**RARITY
RANKINGS**

Overall, Mint State: 47th of 65
High Grade, MS-65 or Finer: 43rd of 65

**LATE-DATE ISSUES
(1941-1947)**
Overall, Mint State: 2nd of 20
High Grade, MS-65 or Finer: 2nd of 20

Important Varieties: None.

General Comments: The 1942-S is the second-rarest, late-date Walking Liberty Half Dollar both from overall and high-grade standpoints. Nevertheless, examples are really not all that difficult to obtain in lower Mint State grades through MS-64. Even MS-65s can be had with relative ease as long as you do not mind owning a coin with noticeable lack of detail. The 1942-S is one of the leading strike rarities in this series, however, and MS-66s are scarce while Superb Gems are nothing short of rare. In fact, fewer than 10 coins have received an MS-67 grade from PCGS and NGC combined (December/2007).

Strike: This is one of the most poorly struck issues in the series. The typical example is flatly struck in the center of the obverse with little, if any detail over Liberty's right (facing) hand, the thigh and the stem of the olive branch. I have seen many examples that are so blunt in that area that the central obverse has an appearance of a plateau in the running down the middle of Liberty's body. Liberty's head and the eagle's breast, trailing leg and shoulder are also softly struck on most 1942-S Half Dollars.

Luster: Luster tends to be vibrant with a frosted texture. A few satiny pieces are also known, but these are not encountered all that often.

Surfaces: The typical example will have a few scattered bagmarks. In general, however, abrasions are not a significant problem for this issue. Remember that it is deficiencies with the strike and not an abundance of abrasions that prevents most 1942-S Half Dollars from grading higher than MS-64.

Toning: There are a few more moderately toned 1942-S Half Dollars in the market than there are for the 1942 or 1942-D. Still, the typical Mint State survivor is either brilliant or lightly toned in iridescent shades. Deeper colors, when present, are usually confined to the peripheries on one or both sides.

Eye Appeal: The 1942-S has below-average eye appeal, an assessment that I attribute entirely to a poorly executed strike.

Significant Examples:

- **NGC MS-67.** *Ex: ANA Charlotte National Money Show Auction (Heritage, 3/2007), lot 1118; Summer FUN Signature Coin Auction (Heritage, 7/2007), lot 1076, where it realized $5,750. The coin did not sell in the first-listed auction.*
- **NGC MS-67.** *Ex: Long Beach, CA Signature Coin Auction (Heritage, 2/2007), lot 4026; CSNS Signature Coin Auction (Heritage, 5/2007), lot 2149, where it realized $9,200. The coin did not sell in the first-listed auction.*
- **NGC MS-67.** *Ex: FUN Signature Sale (Heritage, 1/2005), lot 30258, where it realized $20,700; Robert Moreno Collection (Heritage, 7/2005), lot 10053, where it realized $16,100; ANA Charlotte National Money Show Auction (Heritage, 3/2007), lot 1119, where it realized $4,888.*
- **PCGS MS-67.** *Ex: Long Beach Signature Sale (Heritage, 2/2003), lot 7017, where it realized $25,875.*

Total Known in Mint State: 8,000-9,200+ Coins

TOTAL KNOWN BY GRADE			
MS-60 to MS-63	**MS-64**	**MS-65**	**MS-66 or Finer**
1,350-1,550+ Coins	3,850-4,350 Coins	2,350-2,850 Coins	375-425 Coins

VALUES BY GRADE			
MS-60	**MS-63**	**MS-65**	**MS-67**
$25-$35	$45-$60	$375-$600	$5,000-$30,000+

COLLECTING AND INVESTING STRATEGIES

The leading third-party certification services definitely take strike into consideration when grading 1942-S Walking Liberty Half Dollars. With this fact in mind, and with a suggested strategy to avoid any excessively flat example, I would not purchase a 1942-S that grades lower than MS-65 at PCGS or NGC. Do not expect to find a fully struck coin even in the finer Mint State grades, however, as I cannot recall ever seeing a 1942-S that fits that criterion. Even the PCGS MS-67 in the significant examples list above is a bit softly struck over the highest portion of Liberty's right (facing) hand and along the inside of the eagle's trailing leg. An above-average strike for this issue will include appreciable separation between the thumb and index finger on the right (facing) hand. A boldly-to-sharply struck 1942-S must also display good definition to Liberty's head on the obverse as well as the eagle's breast and shoulder on the reverse.

1943

MINTAGE
53,190,000

RARITY RANKINGS

Overall, Mint State: 65th of 65
High Grade, MS-65 or Finer: 64th of 65

LATE-DATE ISSUES
(1941-1947)

Overall, Mint State: 20th of 20
High Grade, MS-65 or Finer: 19th of 20

Important Varieties: None.

General Comments: The 1943 has the highest mintage in the entire business strike Walking Liberty Half Dollar series. It is the most common issue of the type in terms of total number of Mint State examples known, although the 1946-D is even more plentiful in high grades. Acquiring a coin that falls into the MS-60 to MS-66 grade range is an easy task. MS-67s are moderately scarce in an absolute sense, and they exist in fewer numbers than do those of the 1941. Enough MS-67s have survived, however, that the 1943 is still one of the easiest Walking Liberty Half Dollars to locate in that grade. The same, however, cannot be said for the handful of MS-68s. These are the finest 1943 Half Dollars known to PCGS and NGC (December/2007), and they are very rare coins from a condition standpoint.

Strike: Like other high-mintage Philadelphia Mint issues in this series such as the 1941 and 1942, the 1943 runs the gamut from softly defined to fully struck. Most examples are well produced, however, with at least bold definition over and around Liberty's right (facing) hand. The reverse tends to be even better struck than the obverse, and many examples are free of noteworthy lack of detail even along the inside of the eagle's trailing leg.

Luster: As an issue, the 1943 is highly lustrous with a vibrant, usually frosty mint finish.

Surfaces: This is one of the easier Walking Liberty Half Dollars to locate with overall smooth, if not virtually pristine surfaces.

Toning: The vast majority of Mint State 1943 Half Dollars are fully brilliant with radiant, ice-white surfaces. When present at all, toning is apt to be light with an iridescent quality. In fact, for every moderately-to-heavily toned 1943 that I have seen, at least 10 brilliant and/or lightly toned examples have passed through my hands.

Eye Appeal: The 1943 has strong eye appeal. Indeed, this is one of the more attractive issues in the Walking Liberty Half Dollar series when offered in high grades with sharp-to-full striking detail.

Significant Examples:

- **NGC MS-68.** *Ex: ANA Charlotte National Money Show Auction (Heritage, 3/2007), lot 1120, where it realized $4,600.*
- **PCGS MS-68.** *Ex: Anne Kate Collection (Bowers and Merena, 11/2006), lot 3438, where it realized $12,650.*
- **NGC MS-68.** *Ex: Robert Moreno Collection (Heritage, 7/2005), lot 10054, where it realized $5,463.*
- **PCGS MS-68.** *Ex: Del Rio Collection (Heritage, 8/2004), lot 6573, where it realized $10,350.*
- **NGC MS-68.** *Ex: CSNS Signature Sale (Heritage, 4/2002), lot 5923, where it realized $2,990; Santa Clara Signature Sale (Heritage, 11/2002), lot 6263, where it realized $3,450; November Signature Sale (Heritage, 11/2003), lot 6924, where it realized $3,680.*

Total Known in Mint State: 22,125-25,125+ Coins

TOTAL KNOWN BY GRADE			
MS-60 to MS-63	**MS-64**	**MS-65**	**MS-66 or Finer**
3,200-3,700+ Coins	6,575-7,575+ Coins	8,000-9,000 Coins	4,350-4,850 Coins

VALUES BY GRADE			
MS-60	**MS-63**	**MS-65**	**MS-67**
$25-$30	$35-$40	$100-$150	$300-$650

COLLECTING AND INVESTING STRATEGIES

Take full advantage of the strong eye appeal that this issue possesses and the relatively large number of Superb Gems that have survived by acquiring an example that grades at least MS-67. While boldly and sharply struck coins will also receive an MS-67 or MS-68 grade from PCGS and NGC as long as the surfaces have been expertly preserved, I suggest overlooking those pieces in favor of a fully struck coin. There are just too many 1943 Half Dollars in the market for you not to insist on the utmost in technical quality and eye appeal before making a purchase.

1943-D

MINTAGE
11,346,000

RARITY RANKINGS

***Overall, Mint State:** 48th of 65*
***High Grade, MS-65 or Finer:** 56th of 65*

LATE-DATE ISSUES
(1941-1947)

***Overall, Mint State:** 3rd of 20*
***High Grade, MS-65 or Finer:** 10th of 20*

Important Varieties: None.

General Comments: Along with the 1942-D and 1943-S, the 1943-D is one of the most underrated issues in the late-date Walking Liberty Half Dollar series. In an absolute sense, the 1943-D has a sizeable population in all grades through MS-66. When compared to most other Walking Liberty Half Dollars from the 1940s, however, the population is relatively limited even in lower Mint State grades. MS-67s are scarce, while MS-68s are downright rare.

Strike: A product of the wartime United States Mint, the 1943-D is a high-mintage issue with considerable variation among the striking quality that individual coins possess. The typical example is fairly well struck. Even so, Liberty's right (facing) hand will usually have some degree of softness to the detail. Some coins are quite bluntly defined in the center of the obverse, but I have seen more examples where the highpoint detail in that area is sharp-to-full. Liberty's head and thigh, as well as the eagle's breast and trailing leg feathers, are usually sharply, if not fully struck.

Luster: The 1943-D has very good, if not excellent luster that is almost always frosty in texture.

Surfaces: Scattered abrasions are a problem for many 1943-D Half Dollars, but patience will be rewarded with a more-or-less smooth example that grades MS-65 or finer.

Toning: Brilliant or lightly toned surfaces are the norm for most Mint State 1943-D Half Dollars that you will encounter in the market. There are a few more moderately toned coins for this issue than there are for the 1943, but such pieces are still not encountered all that often.

Eye Appeal: Eye appeal for this issue is above average, if not strong.

Significant Examples:

• **PCGS MS-68.** *Ex: Anne Kate Collection (Bowers and Merena, 11/2006), lot 3441, where it realized $51,175.*

Total Known in Mint State: 8,400-9,700+ Coins

TOTAL KNOWN BY GRADE			
MS-60 to MS-63	**MS-64**	**MS-65**	**MS-66 or Finer**
650-750+ Coins	1,950-2,150 Coins	3,350-3,850 Coins	2,450-2,950 Coins

VALUES BY GRADE			
MS-60	**MS-63**	**MS-65**	**MS-67**
$25-$45	$50-$65	$200-$400	$450-$1,000+

COLLECTING AND INVESTING STRATEGIES

This is one of many issues in the Walking Liberty Half Dollar series for which Cherrypicking will pay dividends. Focus first and foremost on the striking quality over and around Liberty's right (facing) hand in the center of the obverse. There are some sharply-to-fully struck coins intermingled with the typical softly defined examples, and the better-produced pieces are more likely to sell for a strong price when you liquidate your numismatic holdings. I would also avoid coins that grade MS-64 or lower as these tend to be noticeably abraded. The 1943-D is certainly not the most common Walking Liberty Half Dollar in the finer Mint State grades, but enough Gems exist that you should have numerous buying opportunities for such examples in any given year.

1943-S

MINTAGE
13,450,000

RARITY RANKINGS

Overall, Mint State: 49th of 65
High Grade, MS-65 or Finer: 46th of 65

LATE-DATE ISSUES
(1941-1947)

Overall, Mint State: 4th of 20
High Grade, MS-65 or Finer: 4th of 20

Important Varieties: None.

General Comments: In an absolute sense, the 1943-S is a bit more plentiful than the 1943-D. The 1943-S, however, is the rarer of these two issues in high grades. In fact, it is the rarest late-date Walking Liberty Half Dollar in high grades after only the 1941-S, 1942-S and 1944-S. MS-65s are obtainable enough, but MS-66s are moderately scarce due to below-average striking quality for the issue. A Superb Gem 1943-S is a rare coin that does not appear in the market with any degree of frequency.

Strike: As an issue, the 1943-S is only marginally better struck than the 1942-S and 1944-S. The typical example is poorly struck in the center of the obverse. The difference between the 1943-S and, say, the 1942-S is that a poorly struck 1943-S is still likely to have the slightest bit of detail in the center of the obverse. For example, there might be a bit of separation between Liberty's hand and the surrounding gown lines and/or the stem of the olive branch. The worst-struck examples of the 1942-S and 1944-S, on the other hand, are usually completely smooth in the center of the obverse. The 1943-S is also apt to display incomplete detail along the inside of the eagle's trailing leg on the reverse. On the positive side, Liberty's head and the eagle's breast feathers are usually sufficiently bold, if not relatively sharp in definition.

Luster: Contrary to strike, luster quality is a strong suit for this issue. The 1943-S almost always comes highly lustrous with either a frosty or satiny finish.

Surfaces: This can be a difficult issue to locate without at least a few scattered abrasions, but remember that the paucity of high-grade survivors is due primarily to problems with the strike and not excessively abraded surfaces.

Toning: Moderately toned examples are seen once in a while, but the typical 1943-S is either fully brilliant or possessed of only light, iridescent overtones.

Eye Appeal: Since most examples are noticeably soft in striking detail, the 1943-S has below-average eye appeal.

Significant Examples:

- **PCGS MS-67.** *Ex: Denver, CO Signature & Platinum Night Auction (Heritage, 8/2006), lot 3528, where it realized $6,900; ANA Charlotte National Money Show Auction (Heritage, 3/2007), lot 1124, where it realized $6,900.*
- **PCGS MS-67.** *Ex: Anne Kate Collection (Bowers and Merena, 11/2006), lot 3445, where it realized $6,498.*
- **PCGS MS-67.** *Ex: Baltimore Auction (Bowers and Merena, 7/2006), lot 1162, where it realized $8,050.*
- **PCGS MS-67.** *Ex: Baltimore Auction (Bowers and Merena, 12/2004), lot 2195, where it realized $4,600.*
- **PCGS MS-67.** *Ex: Classic Sale (American Numismatic Rarities, 3/2004), lot 663, where it realized $4,140.*
- **PCGS MS-67.** *Ex: ANA Sale of the Millennium (Bowers and Merena, 8/2000), lot 4308, where it realized $2,530.*

Total Known in Mint State: 8,750-9,750+ Coins

TOTAL KNOWN BY GRADE			
MS-60 to MS-63	MS-64	MS-65	MS-66 or Finer
1,400-1,600+ Coins	4,025-4,525 Coins	2,750-2,950 Coins	575-675 Coins

VALUES BY GRADE			
MS-60	MS-63	MS-65	MS-67
$25-$45	$50-$75	$250-$500	$1,750-$8,000+

COLLECTING AND INVESTING STRATEGIES

If you plan to acquire a 100% fully struck 1943-S, prepare instead to be disappointed. I, for one, have never seen such a coin. Even the PCGS and NGC MS-67s that I have encountered have only above-average definition and more-or-less lack of detail over the central obverse highpoint. Your best bet as far as the 1943-S is concerned, therefore, is to select a coin with bold-to-sharp striking detail over and around Liberty's right (facing) hand. Make sure that there is at least some separation between the thumb and index finger on that hand. If you are really persistent you could hold out for an example on which the bottom of the right (facing) hand is well rounded. Many of the better strikes are concentrated at the MS-66 and MS-67 grade levels, so that is where I suggest you target your search.

1944

MINTAGE
28,206,000

RARITY RANKINGS

Overall, Mint State: *58th of 65*
High Grade, MS-65 or Finer: *57th of 65*

LATE-DATE ISSUES
(1941-1947)

Overall, Mint State: *13th of 20*
High Grade, MS-65 or Finer: *12th of 20*

Important Varieties: None.

General Comments: The 1944 is the rarest Philadelphia Mint Half Dollar struck during the Second World War. With a high mintage and good rate of survival, nonetheless, the 1944 is still a readily obtainable coin in all grades from MS-60 through MS-66. Superb Gems are quite rare, however, and the 1944 is unknown any finer than MS-67.

Strike: The 1944 has only average striking quality for a P-mint Half Dollar from the 1940s. The examples that I have seen include many pieces with noticeably soft definition in the center of both the obverse and the reverse. There are enough Mint State examples in the market, however, that persistence will be rewarded with a bold-to-sharp strike that even extends to Liberty's right (facing) hand and the junction of the eagle's breast and right (facing) thigh.

Luster: This issue has excellent luster that is almost always frosty in texture.

Surfaces: The 1944 seldom has trouble with excessively abraded surfaces, and you should have little difficulty locating an overall smooth-looking example.

Toning: The 1944 is more likely to display moderately toned surfaces than the 1941, 1942 or 1943. Nevertheless, a brilliant or lightly toned appearance is still characteristic of most Mint State examples that I have encountered.

Eye Appeal: The 1944 has only average to slightly above-average eye appeal, an assessment that I lay at the feet of inconsistent striking quality. Coins with at least bold definition in and around the center of the obverse, however, are likely to possess strong eye appeal as long as the luster and surface preservation are free of criticism.

Significant Examples:

- **PCGS MS-67.** Ex: Milwaukee, WI ANA Signature Coin Auction (Heritage, 8/2007), lot 1109, where it realized $1,472.
- **PCGS MS-67.** Ex: CSNS Signature Coin Auction (Heritage, 5/2007), lot 3058, where it realized $1,495.
- **PCGS MS-67.** Ex: Pre-Long Beach Coin Auction (Superior, 2/2003), lot 1542, where it realized $4,600; FUN Signature Coin Auction (Heritage, 1/2007), lot 4810. The coin did not sell in the latter auction.
- **PCGS MS-67.** Ex: Dr. Robert W. Swan and Rod Sweet Collections (Bowers and Merena, 3/2004), lot 1623, where it realized $3,220.
- **PCGS MS-67.** Ex: John F. Rindge and Alan J. Harlan Collections (Bowers and Merena, 12/2003), lot 1404, where it realized $3,393.
- **PCGS MS-67.** Ex: Pre-Long Beach Elite Coin Auction (Superior, 5/2003), lot 2686, where it realized $3,738.

Total Known in Mint State: 12,900-14,300+ Coins

TOTAL KNOWN BY GRADE			
MS-60 to MS-63	MS-64	MS-65	MS-66 or Finer
2,100-2,300+ Coins	4,675-5,175+ Coins	4,750-5,250 Coins	1,375-1,575 Coins

VALUES BY GRADE			
MS-60	MS-63	MS-65	MS-67
$25-$30	$35-$40	$120-$200	$1,000-$2,000

COLLECTING AND INVESTING STRATEGIES

As a high-mintage Philadelphia Mint issue from the 1940s, the 1944 is often regarded as an easy coin to locate with strong technical quality and eye appeal. I believe that collectors and investors that subscribe to this view are making a mistake. It is my firm belief that you should approach this issue with a very critical eye lest you end up purchasing a coin with below-average quality. Pay special attention to the striking detail over and around Liberty's right (facing) hand in the center of the obverse. Many 1944 Half Dollars are softly struck in that area. You will be maximizing your investment potential for this issue if you insist on acquiring an example with sharp detail in all areas. Such coins do exist, and they can be found in all Mint State grades from MS-60 to MS-67. My personal preference, of course, is for coins that grade MS-65 or finer that have few, if any, distracting abrasions and full, vibrant mint luster.

1944-D

MINTAGE
9,769,000

**RARITY
RANKINGS**

Overall, Mint State: 52nd of 65
High Grade, MS-65 or Finer: 58th of 65

**LATE-DATE ISSUES
(1941-1947)**
Overall, Mint State: 7th of 20
High Grade, MS-65 or Finer: 13th of 20

Important Varieties: A variety is known where the designer's initials were omitted from the original reverse die and later added by hand. The attribution for this variety is FS-901.

General Comments: The 1944-D is a plentiful issue in an absolute sense that is easily obtainable in all grades through MS-66. Superb Gems are scarce-to-rare, however, and most are confined to the MS-67 grade level. Additionally, the 1944-D is rarer than the 1945-D, 1946-D or 1946-S in terms of total number of Mint State coins known.

Strike: The 1944-D is similar in striking quality to the 1943-D. The typical example lacks full detail on Liberty's right (facing) hand in the center of the obverse. Many coins are actually quite blunt in that area, although others are relatively sharp. The gown lines over Liberty's thigh are also sometimes softly defined. On the other hand, Liberty's head, the eagle's breast and the inside of the eagle's trailing leg tend to be sharp-to-full in detail.

Luster: Luster for this issue is excellent and usually of a frosty texture. Satiny examples are also known, but they are in the minority among the Mint State examples that I have seen.

Surfaces: Surface preservation varies from noticeably abraded to virtually pristine. The typical 1944-D has a few scattered abrasions, but you should be able to locate an overall smooth example without undue effort.

Toning: The vast majority of 1944-D Half Dollars available in the market are either brilliant or lightly toned with iridescent highlights. When present at all, deeper colors are usually confined to the peripheries on one or both sides of the coin. The few examples that I have seen with moderate toning throughout are quite attractive, and it is a shame that there are not more of those coins from which to choose.

Eye Appeal: The 1944-D has above-average, if not strong eye appeal.

Significant Examples:

   • **NGC MS-68.** *Ex: Nevada Silver Collection; Pre-Long Beach Elite Coin Auction (Superior, 5/2003), lot 2687, where it realized $13,800; Robert Moreno Collection (Heritage, 7/2005), lot 10058, where it realized $18,975; ANA Charlotte National Money Show Auction (Heritage, 3/2007), lot 1133, where it realized $8,050.*

Total Known in Mint State: 10,225-11,825+ Coins

TOTAL KNOWN BY GRADE			
MS-60 to MS-63	**MS-64**	**MS-65**	**MS-66 or Finer**
850-950+ Coins	2,700-3,200+ Coins	4,325-4,825 Coins	2,350-2,850 Coins

VALUES BY GRADE			
MS-60	**MS-63**	**MS-65**	**MS-67**
$25-$35	$40-$60	$150-$250	$550-$1,000+

COLLECTING AND INVESTING STRATEGIES

As with the 1943-D, the 1944-D is an issue that you should Cherrypick for strike. Insist on sharp detail over and around Liberty's right (facing) hand that includes good separation to the index finger and thumb. Coins that fit this criterion are scattered throughout the MS-60 to MS-67 grade range, so exactly which grade you choose should depend on your tolerance for abrasions and the size of your numismatic budget. If funds permit, try to acquire a coin that grades at least MS-65. Be selective as far as surface preservation is concerned as I have seen some MS-65s with one or two relatively sizeable abrasions that can be distracting to the naked eye. MS-66s and MS-67s, of course, should be virtually abrasion free.

1944-S

MINTAGE
8,904,000

RARITY RANKINGS

Overall, Mint State: *53rd of 65*
High Grade, MS-65 or Finer: *44th of 65*

**LATE-DATE ISSUES
(1941-1947)**

Overall, Mint State: *8th of 20*
High Grade, MS-65 or Finer: *3rd of 20*

Important Varieties: Two Repunched Mintmark varieties are known, and there is another variety on which the S mintmark was punched into the die upside down. The attributions for these varieties are FS-501, FS-502/Fox V-101 and FS-511, respectively.

General Comments: The 1944-S is an easy issue to obtain through the MS-65 grade level so long as you do not mind acquiring a coin with poor striking detail. Due to this deficiency, many smooth, if not virtually pristine examples cannot grade any finer than MS-64 or MS-65 at PCGS and NGC. As such, the 1944-S is scarce in MS-66 and exceedingly rare as a Superb Gem. Among the late-date issues in this series, only the 1941-S and 1942-S are rarer than the 1944-S in high grades. The 1944-S is also rarer in high grades than the 1936, 1939, 1939-D and 1940.

Strike: A leading strike rarity in the Walking Liberty Half Dollar series, the 1944-S typically displays very little definition in the center of the obverse. Most coins are completely smooth in that area with no separation between Liberty's right (facing) hand, the thigh and the stem of the olive branch. The eagle's breast and trailing leg feathers are also apt to be softly defined, but lack of detail in those areas is usually less conspicuous than in the center of the obverse. Liberty's head can also be bluntly defined, although many examples that are poorly struck in the center of the obverse are sharply impressed over the head.

Luster: A redeeming factor for many poorly struck 1944-S Half Dollars, the issue as a whole comes with vibrant luster that can be either satiny or fully frosted in texture.

Surfaces: Abrasions are generally not a problem for this issue, and it is not that difficult to locate a coin with overall smooth-looking surfaces.

Toning: Brilliant or lightly toned surfaces are the norm for this issue, although I have seen the occasional example with deeper, more vivid colors at the rims.

Eye Appeal: Despite having excellent luster quality and no real problems with abrasions, the 1944-S has below-average eye appeal due to poor striking quality and noticeable lack of detail in prime focal areas.

Significant Examples:

• **NGC MS-67.** *Ex: ANA Charlotte National Money Show Auction (Heritage, 3/2007), lot 1136, where it realized $5,175.*

• **NGC MS-67.** *Ex: Robert Moreno Collection (Heritage, 7/2005), lot 10059; Dallas, TX Signature Auction (Heritage, 11/2005), lot 2179, where it realized $9,775. The coin did not sell in the first-listed auction.*

• **PCGS MS-67.** *Ex: CSNS Signature Auction (Heritage, 5/2005), lot 7493, where it realized $20,700.*

• **PCGS MS-67.** *Ex: Long Beach Sale (Heritage, 10/2000), lot 6315, where it realized $8,050; Ally Collection (Heritage, 8566, where it realized $12,650.*

Total Known in Mint State: 10,200-11,950+ Coins

TOTAL KNOWN BY GRADE			
MS-60 to MS-63	**MS-64**	**MS-65**	**MS-66 or Finer**
1,975-2,175+ Coins	5,225-6,225 Coins	2,625-3,125 Coins	375-425 Coins

VALUES BY GRADE			
MS-60	**MS-63**	**MS-65**	**MS-67**
$25-$35	$40-$60	$300-$500	$5,000-$20,000+

COLLECTING AND INVESTING STRATEGIES

I have never seen a 1944-S with 100% full striking detail, but I have seen examples with above-average detail in the center of the obverse. The best strikes are largely concentrated at the MS-67 grade level. However, absent considerable patience and fairly deep pockets, the rarity and consequent cost of such coins will preclude you from buying a Superb Gem 1944-S. MS-66s, on the other hand, trade much more frequently and are more affordable at an average cost of $800-$1,200. Do not expect miracles with the strike on a 1944-S in MS-66, however, as most examples will still lack separation between the thumb and index finger on Liberty's right (facing) hand. What you will be gaining in an MS-66 as opposed to the typical lower-grade example is some distinction between Liberty's right (facing) hand, her thigh and the stem of the olive branch. A 1944-S with at least that degree of striking detail in the center of the obverse, as well as sharp definition to Liberty's head and the eagle's breast, will provide the strongest possible return on your investment in this challenging issue.

1945

MINTAGE
31,502,000

RARITY RANKINGS

Overall, Mint State: 62nd of 65
High Grade, MS-65 or Finer: 59th of 65

LATE-DATE ISSUES
(1941-1947)

Overall, Mint State: 17th of 20
High Grade, MS-65 or Finer: 14th of 20

Important Varieties: There is a very interesting variety of the 1945 Half Dollar that lacks the designer's initials at the lower-right reverse border. It is attributed as FS-901, Fox V-102 and Breen-5211.

General Comments: Mint State examples abound in the market, although they are not quite as plentiful as those of the 1942, 1943 or 1946-D. The majority of Mint State 1945 Half Dollars are concentrated in the MS-60 to MS-66 grade range. For an issue that is so plentiful in lower grades, the 1945 is surprisingly elusive as a Superb Gem. There are fewer than 125 MS-67s known, and the MS-68 listed at PCGS is the only 1945 Half Dollar to have received that grade from both major grading services (December/2007).

Strike: The 1945 ranges from bold to full in striking detail, and sharply struck examples are seen on a regular basis in the market. When present, lack of detail is usually minor and confined to Liberty's head, right (facing) hand and/or the inside of the eagle's trailing leg.

Luster: Luster quality for this issue is very good, if not excellent and the typical example has a richly frosted texture.

Surfaces: Locating an overall smooth or virtually pristine 1945 Half Dollar is a fairly easy task by the standards of the Walking Liberty series.

Toning: The majority of Mint State examples are brilliant. Interestingly, toned coins tend to have a moderate amount of patina on both sides as opposed to light, iridescent overtones. If present, vivid colors such as red and orange are usually confined to the peripheries. There is an exception to this, however, and it is a group of 1945 Half Dollars with deep, rich, orange-copper patina that touches most areas. I began encountering these coins in the mid-to-late 1990s, and they were almost always certified by NGC. It is my belief that a small number (perhaps even a single roll) of Mint State 1945 Half Dollars with distinct toning surfaced around that time and was sent to NGC for certification before being dispersed into the market.

Eye Appeal: The 1945 has strong eye appeal, and a high-grade example with well-preserved surfaces is an attractive representative of the type.

Significant Examples: The finest 1945 Half Dollar known to PCGS and NGC is an MS-68 at the former service (December/2007). I am unaware of an auction sale for that coin during the eight-year period from 2000-2007.

Total Known in Mint State: 18,000-20,000+ Coins

TOTAL KNOWN BY GRADE			
MS-60 to MS-63	**MS-64**	**MS-65**	**MS-66 or Finer**
2,875-3,275+ Coins	6,400-6,900+ Coins	6,725-7,225 Coins	2,050-2,550 Coins

VALUES BY GRADE			
MS-60	**MS-63**	**MS-65**	**MS-67**
$25-$30	$35-$40	$100-$175	$1,000-$2,000

COLLECTING AND INVESTING STRATEGIES

For a common Walking Liberty Half Dollar such as this, you would be best served by emphasizing eye appeal over investment potential when the time comes to buy. Rest assured that if you select a high-grade, attractive coin with a sharp strike and no singularly distracting abrasions, you will also be doing all within your power to guarantee a strong return on your investment in an example of this issue.

1945-D

MINTAGE
9,966,800

RARITY RANKINGS

Overall, Mint State: 59th of 65
High Grade, MS-65 or Finer: 61st of 65

LATE-DATE ISSUES
(1941-1947)

Overall, Mint State: 14th of 20
High Grade, MS-65 or Finer: 16th of 20

Important Varieties: None.

General Comments: Another high-mintage issue from the World War Two era, the 1945-D is an easy find in all grades from MS-60 to MS-66. MS-67s are scarce when viewed in the wider context of the numismatic market, but they are plentiful for a Denver Mint issue in this series. Rarer than the 1941, 1942, 1943, 1945, 1946-D and 1946-S in terms of total number of Mint State examples known, the 1945-D is by no means the most common Walking Liberty Half Dollar. There is a lone MS-68 listed at NGC (December/2007).

Strike: The 1945-D was struck to a higher standard of quality than any other Denver Mint Walking Liberty Half Dollar from 1941-1945. Examples are rarely encountered with less than bold definition, and I have seen plenty of coins with a sharp or virtually full strike that even extends to Liberty's right (facing) hand in the center of the obverse.

Luster: The typical 1945-D has excellent luster with a frosty texture to both sides. Satiny examples are encountered less frequently, but even those coins usually have appealing luster.

Surfaces: This issue is usually offered with surfaces that are smooth in overall appearance and seldom displays more than a few scattered abrasions.

Toning: There is a nearly 50-50 mix of brilliant and lightly toned examples among extant 1945-D Half Dollars. The toned coins tend to have iridescent overtones in colors such as gold, silver and pink. Moderately toned examples, or those with more vivid colors at the rims, are also known but can be elusive from a market availability standpoint.

Eye Appeal: Eye appeal for this issue is nothing short of strong.

Significant Examples:

> • **NGC MS-68.** *Ex: CSNS Signature Coin Auction (Heritage, 5/2007), lot 3064; Summer FUN Signature Coin Auction (Heritage, 7/2007), lot 1082; Long Beach, CA Signature Coin Auction (Heritage, 9/2007), lot 1778, where it realized $7,763. The coin did not sell in either of the first two auction appearances.*

Total Known in Mint State: 14,000-16,200+ Coins

TOTAL KNOWN BY GRADE			
MS-60 to MS-63	**MS-64**	**MS-65**	**MS-66 or Finer**
975-1,175+ Coins	3,750-4,250+ Coins	6,425-7,425 Coins	2,850-3,350 Coins

VALUES BY GRADE			
MS-60	**MS-63**	**MS-65**	**MS-67**
$20-$25	$30-$50	$110-$160	$625-$1,250+

COLLECTING AND INVESTING STRATEGIES

A well-produced and carefully preserved issue, the 1945-D should be easy to obtain with a sharp-to-full strike, vibrant luster and smooth-looking surfaces. You should acquire an example that grades at least MS-65 in order to best appreciate the strong technical quality and eye appeal for which this issue is known.

1945-S

MINTAGE
10,156,000

**RARITY
RANKINGS**

Overall, Mint State: 57th of 65
High Grade, MS-65 or Finer: 53rd of 65

**LATE-DATE ISSUES
(1941-1947)**
Overall, Mint State: 12th of 20
High Grade, MS-65 or Finer: 8th of 20

Important Varieties: None.

General Comments: The 1945-S is a median rarity among late-date Walking Liberty Half Dollars. It is rarer than issues such as the 1945-D, 1946-D and 1946-S, but easier to obtain than others like the 1942-S, 1943-S and 1944-S. Still, examples that grade MS-60 to MS-65 are available with ease. Even MS-66s are plentiful enough that you should have no difficulty acquiring one. Superb Gems, however, are rare.

Strike: The 1945-S is akin to the 1943-S in that it has a slightly better strike than the 1942-S and 1944-S. The typical example, nevertheless, is flatly struck in the center of the obverse with essentially no detail to Liberty's right (facing) hand. Liberty's head is also noticeably soft on many examples. The reverse tends to come with overall bolder definition and, at most, only minimal softness of detail over the eagle's breast and along the inside of the trailing leg.

Luster: This issue has excellent luster that can be either satiny or frosty in finish.

Surfaces: When present on an example of this issue, abrasions tend to be few in number and not overly distracting. A fair number of 1945-S Half Dollars are overall smooth in appearance.

Toning: The typical example is brilliant or, at most, minimally toned. Most toned 1945-S Half Dollars have either light, iridescent color throughout or deeper colors that are confined to the peripheries.

Eye Appeal: Due to deficiencies with the strike, the 1945-S has slightly below-average eye appeal.

Significant Examples:

- **NGC MS-67.** *Ex: ANA Charlotte National Money Show Auction (Heritage, 3/2007), lot 1143, where it realized $1,380.*
- **NGC MS-67.** *Ex: Dallas Signature Coin Auction (Heritage, 10/2006), lot 2146, where it realized $2,300.*
- **NGC MS-67.** *Ex: Robert Moreno Collection (Heritage, 7/2005), lot 10063; Dallas, TX Signature Auction (Heritage, 11/2005), lot 2911, where it realized $1,840. The coin did not sell in the first-listed auction.*
- **NGC MS-67.** *Ex: Mandalay Bay Rarities Sale (Bowers and Merena, 10/2004), lot 387. The coin did not sell in that auction appearance.*

Total Known in Mint State: 12,000-13,900+ Coins

TOTAL KNOWN BY GRADE			
MS-60 to MS-63	**MS-64**	**MS-65**	**MS-66 or Finer**
1,650-1,850+ Coins	5,075-6,075 Coins	4,375-4,875 Coins	900-1,100 Coins

VALUES BY GRADE			
MS-60	**MS-63**	**MS-65**	**MS-67**
$25-$35	$40-$60	$125-$225	$1,750-$15,000+

COLLECTING AND INVESTING STRATEGIES

Do not expect to find a 1945-S with 100% full striking detail. On the other hand, I do not recommend that you rush out and purchase the first example that fits into your price range. If you follow that strategy, odds are that you will end up with a poorly struck example. A much better strategy is to search for a coin with at least the slightest bit of separation between the bottom of Liberty's right (facing) hand and her thigh, as well as between the folds of the gown and the stem of the olive branch in that hand. I would be even more selective as far as Liberty's head and the eagle's breast feathers are concerned; make sure that they are bold-to-sharp in detail. You can go as low as MS-64 and still find a 1945-S with these striking characteristics, but be wary of the detail to Liberty's head and the eagle's breast on coins that grade lower than MS-66.

1946

MINTAGE
12,118,000

RARITY RANKINGS

Overall, Mint State: 54th of 65
High Grade, MS-65 or Finer: 52nd of 65

LATE-DATE ISSUES
(1941-1947)

Overall, Mint State: 9th of 20
High Grade, MS-65 or Finer: 7th of 20

Important Varieties: There is both a Doubled Die Obverse and a Doubled Die Reverse variety of the 1946 Walking Liberty Half Dollar. The DDO is attributed as FS-101. The DDR, which is more visually dramatic, goes by the attributions FS-801, Fox V-101 and Breen-5215.

General Comments: An underrated issue, the 1946 is the rarest Walking Liberty Half Dollar struck in the Philadelphia Mint from 1941 through 1947. In an absolute sense, however, this issue is still readily obtainable in all grades through MS-66. Superb Gems are surprisingly rare when you consider the large number of coins struck.

Strike: This is a well-produced issue, and the typical example is boldly, if not sharply struck from the dies. I have even seen quite a few coins with full striking detail.

Luster: The 1946 has very good luster quality, the coins usually displaying a frosty texture to the mint finish.

Surfaces: This is a more challenging issue to locate with overall smooth surfaces than you might expect for a Philadelphia Mint Walking Liberty Half Dollar from the 1940s. Still, the typical 1946 has only a few scattered bagmarks on one or both sides, and I have not seen all that many examples with excessively abraded surfaces.

Toning: Brilliant or lightly toned surfaces are seen on most Mint State survivors of this issue. A few examples have deeper colors, but usually only at the rims.

Eye Appeal: The 1946 has strong eye appeal.

Significant Examples:

• **NGC MS-68★.** *Ex: Portland, OR Signature Sale (Heritage, 3/2004), lot 5912, where it realized $14,950; Robert Moreno Collection (Heritage, 7/2005), lot 10065, where it realized $18,400.*

• **PCGS MS-66.** *Ex: Lincoln Sale (Kingswood, 1/2003), lot 469, where it realized $5,750. This coin is an example of the Doubled Die Reverse variety FS-50-1946-801.*

Total Known in Mint State: 10,675-12,075+ Coins

TOTAL KNOWN BY GRADE			
MS-60 to MS-63	**MS-64**	**MS-65**	**MS-66 or Finer**
1,625-1,825+ Coins	4,275-4,775 Coins	3,750-4,250 Coins	1,025-1,225 Coins

VALUES BY GRADE			
MS-60	**MS-63**	**MS-65**	**MS-67**
$20-$30	$35-$55	$125-$175	$1,250-$5,000

COLLECTING AND INVESTING STRATEGIES

Be wary of the occasional 1946 Half Dollar with slight incompleteness of detail over Liberty's head, her right (facing) hand and/or the eagle's trailing leg feathers. Avoid these coins and focus on acquiring one of the many sharply-to-fully struck examples in the market.

1946-D

MINTAGE
2,151,000

**RARITY
RANKINGS**

Overall, Mint State: 63rd of 65
High Grade, MS-65 or Finer: 65th of 65

**LATE-DATE ISSUES
(1941-1947)**

Overall, Mint State: 18th of 20
High Grade, MS-65 or Finer: 20th of 20

Important Varieties: None.

General Comments: Despite a much lower mintage, the 1946-D is considerably more common than the 1946 in Mint State. Some might argue that the lower mintage and, hence, greater desirability of the 1946-D makes it more conducive to third-party certification than the 1946. I do not agree with this argument because the 1946-D has a significantly larger certified population in MS-65 and MS-66 – two of the grades where numismatic premiums make it likely that both issues would see equally widespread submission to PCGS and NGC. If the 1946 were more common than the 1946-D, I would expect to see a greater number of coins certified in MS-65 than for the 1946-D.

The 1946-D is readily obtainable in all grades through MS-66, and it is the most common Walking Liberty Half Dollar in high grades. MS-67s are still scarce in an absolute sense, however, and the issue is unknown any finer.

Strike: The average strike for this issue will be more-or-less soft over Liberty's head, the right (facing) hand and, to a lesser extent, the eagle's breast and trailing leg feathers. Nevertheless, there are many boldly and sharply struck examples of the 1946-D in the market and it is actually quite easy to find with virtually full detail on the reverse.

Luster: The 1946-D has very good-to-excellent luster that can have either a satin or frosty texture.

Surfaces: Abrasions are seldom a significant impediment to locating an attractive 1946-D.

Toning: Brilliant-to-lightly toned surfaces are the norm for this issue. Moderately toned coins are not seen all that often, and the toning on such coins is either confined to the peripheries or equally distributed across the surfaces.

Eye Appeal: The 1946-D has above-average eye appeal, and sharply struck examples rate even higher in this regard.

Significant Examples:

- **PCGS MS-67.** *Ex: Milwaukee, WI ANA Signature Coin Auction (Heritage, 8/2007), lot 1112, where it realized $1,956.*
- **NGC MS-67.** *Ex: Vanek Collection (Heritage, 7/2007), lot 1084, where it realized $863.*
- **PCGS MS-67.** *Ex: ANA Charlotte National Money Show Auction (Heritage, 3/2007), lot 1147, where it realized $2,530.*
- **PCGS MS-67.** *Ex: Denver ANA Auction (Bowers and Merena, 8/2006), lot 3569, where it realized $2,128.*
- **PCGS MS-67.** *Ex: Intervale Sale (Kingswood, 1/2002), lot 442, where it realized $3,105.*
- **NGC MS-67.** *Ex: Pre-Long Beach Sale (Superior, 5/2001), lot 3569, where it realized $1,553.*

Total Known in Mint State: 20,850-24,250+ Coins

TOTAL KNOWN BY GRADE			
MS-60 to MS-63	**MS-64**	**MS-65**	**MS-66 or Finer**
1,250-1,450+ Coins	6,550-7,550 Coins	10,650-12,650 Coins	2,400-2,600 Coins

VALUES BY GRADE			
MS-60	**MS-63**	**MS-65**	**MS-67**
$30-$35	$40-$60	$100-$150	$900-$2,750

COLLECTING AND INVESTING STRATEGIES

The large number of Mint State 1946-D Half Dollars relative to the reported mintage figure cannot be explained any other way than through widespread hoarding. Indeed, I believe that many coins were set aside at the time of issue by dealers, speculators and even possibly some collectors who believed that a limited mintage would eventually translate into a significant numismatic premium. This has really not happened except in circulated grades, and it seems that little hoarding of worn coins has taken place over the years. While I do not dislike the 1946-D, I would not get overly excited when an example is offered for sale. There are thousands of Mint State coins from which to choose, and they tend to come well preserved with vibrant luster and a minimum number of abrasions. Boldly-to-sharply struck examples are also relatively plentiful among the survivors. If you are debating between purchasing an attractive 1946-D and an above-average example of an issue such as the 1942-S, 1944-S or even the 1943-D, pass on the 1946-D in favor of the other coin. Appealing, high-quality examples are in much greater supply for this issue than they are for most other mintmarked Walking Liberty Halves from the 1940s.

1946-S

MINTAGE
3,724,000

RARITY RANKINGS

Overall, Mint State: 60th of 65
High Grade, MS-65 or Finer: 60th of 65

**LATE-DATE ISSUES
(1941-1947)**

Overall, Mint State: 15th of 20
High Grade, MS-65 or Finer: 15th of 20

Important Varieties: None.

General Comments: The 1946-S is the most common San Francisco Mint issue in the entire Walking Liberty Half Dollar series, although it is not quite as plentiful as the 1941, 1942, 1943 or 1946-D. This issue is easy to obtain in all grades through MS-66. MS-67s are quite rare, however, and there are no coins certified finer at either PCGS or NGC (December/2007).

Strike: Most 1946-S Half Dollars are softly struck in the center of the obverse over and around Liberty's right (facing) hand, and the typical example is quite blunt in that area. Liberty's head is also apt to display noteworthy lack of definition. The reverse is usually better produced than the obverse, but softness of detail over the eagle's breast and/or trailing leg feathers is still a problem for many examples. The 1946-S is far from the worst-struck issue in the Walking Liberty Half Dollar series, however, and the quality of strike is a marginal improvement over that of wartime issues such as the 1942-S, 1943-S, 1944-S and 1945-S.

Luster: Like the other San Francisco Mint Walking Liberty Half Dollars from the 1940s, the 1946-S is a highly lustrous issue. Most coins that I have seen have a frosty finish, but there are also plenty of satiny examples known.

Surfaces: The typical 1946-S has few, if any distracting abrasions. This is a relatively easy issue to locate with overall smooth, if not virtually pristine surfaces.

Toning: The vast majority of Mint State 1946-S Half Dollars are either fully brilliant or lightly toned in iridescent shades of gold, silver and/or pinkish colors. As with most other issues from the mid-to-late 1940s, deeper, more vivid toning on a 1946-S is apt to be confined to the peripheries.

Eye Appeal: Although the 1946-S is seldom encountered with a sharp strike in all areas, the issue still has slightly above-average eye appeal. Vibrant luster and an overall lack of distracting abrasions among Mint State survivors are desirable attributes, and the overall definition is a bit better than that seen on leading strike rarities in this series such as the 1942-S and 1944-S.

Significant Examples:

- **PCGS MS-67.** *Ex: CSNS Signature Coin Auction (Heritage, 5/2007), lot 3070, where it realized $6,613.*
- **PCGS MS-67.** *Ex: ANA Charlotte National Money Show Auction (Heritage, 3/2007), lot 1149, where it realized $6,900.*
- **NGC MS-67.** *Ex: ANA Charlotte National Money Show Auction (Heritage, 3/2007), lot 1150, where it realized $1,265.*
- **NGC MS-67.** *Ex: Nevada Silver Collection; FUN Signature Coin Auction (Heritage, 1/2007), lot 4820, where it realized $1,495.*
- **NGC MS-67★.** *Ex: Dallas Signature Coin Auction (Heritage, 11/2006), lot 1001, where it realized $2,070.*

Total Known in Mint State: 14,600-16,500+ Coins

TOTAL KNOWN BY GRADE			
MS-60 to MS-63	**MS-64**	**MS-65**	**MS-66 or Finer**
1,025-1,225+ Coins	4,650-5,150 Coins	6,975-7,975 Coins	1,950-2,150 Coins

VALUES BY GRADE			
MS-60	**MS-63**	**MS-65**	**MS-67**
$25-$35	$40-$50	$100-$200	$1,250-$7,500

COLLECTING AND INVESTING STRATEGIES

While the typical 1946-S is softly defined in one or more areas, it is still possible to locate a coin with overall bold-to-sharp striking detail. Persistence is a prerequisite for adopting this strategy, as the best-struck examples are in fairly short supply, and many are already sequestered in tightly held collections or investment portfolios. For a more relaxed search, you could settle for a coin with some degree of separation between the index finger and thumb on Liberty's right (facing) hand. However, to maximize your investment potential in this issue, I suggest acquiring an MS-66 or MS-67 with considerably more definition over and around Liberty's right (facing) hand. Look for a coin on which the hand is distinct from the thigh and the stem of the olive branch. Examples that meet that criterion are usually (but not always!) sufficiently struck over Liberty's head and the eagle's breast.

1947

MINTAGE
4,094,000

RARITY RANKINGS

Overall, Mint State: 56th of 65
High Grade, MS-65 or Finer: 54th of 65

LATE-DATE ISSUES
(1941-1947)

Overall, Mint State: 11th of 20
High Grade, MS-65 or Finer: 9th of 20

Important Varieties: None.

General Comments: The final Philadelphia Mint issue in the Walking Liberty Half Dollar series, the 1947 is an underrated coin much like the 1946. It is rarer than the 1941, 1942, 1943, 1944 and 1945, as well as the 1941-D, 1943-D, 1944-D, 1945-D, 1946-D and 1946-S in high grades. You should still have little difficulty locating an example that falls into the MS-60 to MS-66 grade range, although MS-66s are a bit scarce from a market availability standpoint. Superb Gems are rare, and none grade finer than MS-67 at either PCGS or NGC (December/2007).

Strike: This is not one of the better-produced Philadelphia Mint Walking Liberty Half Dollars from the 1940s. Many examples have noticeable softness of detail over Liberty's head and/or right (facing) hand. Striking quality does vary, however, and it is possible to locate a sharply-to-fully struck 1947 without too much effort. The reverse is usually better produced than the obverse. Even coins that are softly impressed in the center of the obverse tend to be quite sharp over the eagle's plumage.

Luster: Luster quality for this issue is free of criticism, and most examples are quite vibrant with either a satin or frosty finish.

Surfaces: The 1947 is a generally well-preserved issue, and the typical Mint State survivor is either minimally abraded or free of noteworthy bagmarks.

Toning: I have seen a few more richly toned examples of the 1947 than I have for such other Half Dollars from the 1940s as the 1944, 1945 and 1946. Nevertheless, the typical Mint State example is either fully brilliant or lightly toned in iridescent shades. Moderately-to-extensively toned examples tend to be highly attractive with vivid colors.

Eye Appeal: Eye appeal is usually very strong for this issue, but coins with noticeable lack of highpoint definition on the obverse are only above average in this regard.

Significant Examples:

• **NGC MS-67.** *Ex: Orlando Rarities Sale (Bowers and Merena, 1/2008), lot 269, where it realized $1,610.*

• **NGC MS-67★.** *Ex: CSNS Signature Coin Auction (Heritage, 5/2007), lot 3071, where it realized $1,737.*

• **PCGS MS-67.** *Ex: ANA Charlotte National Money Show Auction (Heritage, 3/2007), lot 1151, where it realized $6,900.*

• **PCGS MS-67.** *Ex: GBW; Temecula Collection (Heritage, 1/2007), lot 1017, where it realized $8,338.*

• **NGC MS-67.** *Ex: John F. Rindge and Alan J. Harlan Collections (Bowers and Merena, 12/2003), lot 1419, where it realized $3,105.*

• **NGC MS-67.** *Ex: Pre-Long Beach Auction (Ira & Larry Goldberg, 2/2003), lot 654, where it realized $2,530.*

Total Known in Mint State: 11,600-13,000+ Coins

TOTAL KNOWN BY GRADE			
MS-60 to MS-63	**MS-64**	**MS-65**	**MS-66 or Finer**
1,500-1,700+ Coins	4,650-5,150 Coins	4,250-4,750 Coins	1,150-1,350 Coins

VALUES BY GRADE			
MS-60	**MS-63**	**MS-65**	**MS-67**
$25-$35	$40-$50	$125-$200	$1,250-$8,500

COLLECTING AND INVESTING STRATEGIES

Avoid any 1947 Half Dollar with below-average striking detail that includes noticeable softness to Liberty's head and/or right (facing) hand. Sharply and fully struck coins are definitely available, so do not be afraid to pass over the first few coins that you encounter if the overall definition is not up to a high standard.

1947-D

MINTAGE
3,900,600

**RARITY
RANKINGS**

Overall, Mint State: 55th of 65
High Grade, MS-65 or Finer: 51st of 65

**LATE-DATE ISSUES
(1941-1947)**

Overall, Mint State: 10th of 20
High Grade, MS-65 or Finer: 6th of 20

Important Varieties: None.

General Comments: The 1947-D is easier to obtain than the 1947 in most Mint State grades. It is, however, rarer than the 1941-D, 1943-D, 1944-D, 1945-D and 1946-D in high grades. Expect little difficulty locating Mint State coins through MS-65. Although the 1947-D is equally as scarce as the 1947 in MS-66, you should be able to locate an example in that grade without too much effort. Superb Gems are rare.

Strike: The 1947-D is a generally well-struck issue, and many examples that I have seen are sharply defined. Liberty's right (facing) hand is sometimes a tad soft, however, but Liberty's head and the eagle's breast seldom have this problem.

Luster: This is a highly lustrous issue that almost always displays a frosty texture to the mint finish.

Surfaces: The 1947-D is fairly easy to locate with an overall smooth-looking appearance, and coins with more than a few scattered abrasions are quite rare among Mint State survivors.

Toning: Most examples have some degree of toning, even if it is only light with an iridescent quality. Moderately toned examples are seen quite regularly, sometimes with deeper patina confined only to the rims. The 1947-D is not one of the easier Walking Liberty Half Dollars from the 1940s to locate with fully brilliant surfaces.

Eye Appeal: Eye appeal for this issue is generally above average, although your final assessment of a moderately toned example is likely to depend on what you think of the shade and/or distribution of the color(s).

Significant Examples:

- **NGC MS-67.** *Ex: CSNS Signature Coin Auction (Heritage, 5/2007), lot 3073, where it realized $1,380.*
- **PCGS MS-67.** *Ex: ANA Charlotte National Money Show Auction (Heritage, 3/2007), lot 1153, where it realized $8,800.*
- **NGC MS-67.** *Ex: ANA Charlotte National Money Show Auction (Heritage, 3/2007), lot 1154, where it realized $1,121.*
- **PCGS MS-67.** *Ex: Long Beach, CA Signature Coin Auction (Heritage, 2/2007), lot 4047, where it realized $9,890.*
- **NGC MS-67.** *Ex: New York Invitational Sale (David Lawrence, 7/2004), lot 3176, where it realized $1,380.*
- **NGC MS-67.** *Ex: "Elite" Sale (Superior, 1/2002), lot 1172, where it realized $2,990.*

Total Known in Mint State: 11,000-12,800+ Coins

TOTAL KNOWN BY GRADE			
MS-60 to MS-63	**MS-64**	**MS-65**	**MS-66 or Finer**
1,175-1,375+ Coins	5,050-6,050 Coins	3,475-3,975 Coins	1,250-1,450 Coins

VALUES BY GRADE			
MS-60	**MS-63**	**MS-65**	**MS-67**
$25-$35	$45-$55	$100-$200	$1,000-$10,000

COLLECTING AND INVESTING STRATEGIES

If you are patient and selective with your numismatic purchases, you should have little difficulty locating a sharply, if not fully struck 1947-D Half Dollar to include among your numismatic holdings. Toning is another matter entirely. You might have to wait longer than anticipated for the opportunity to purchase a coin that is completely free of toning with blast-white surfaces. On the other hand, the 1947-D should be an enjoyable issue to pursue if you are a fan of richly original toning. Many examples have vivid colors, and these are usually highly attractive. I would avoid coins with overly splotchy toning as that feature can be distracting to many buyers and, thus, might hurt your chances of obtaining a strong price when the time comes to sell.

Rarity Summary for
Proof Walking Liberty Half Dollars:
1936-1942

OVERALL RARITY		
Rank	Issue	Coins Known
1	1936	1,600-1,850
2	1937	2,000-2,350
3	1938	2,250-2,575
4	1939	2,500-2,900
5	1940	3,000-3,350
6	1941	3,900-4,500
7	1942	5,450-6,400

HIGH-GRADE RARITY, PROOF-65 OR FINER		
Rank	Issue	Coins Known
1	1936	835-935
2	1937	1,250-1,450
3	1938	1,550-1,750
4	1939	1,875-2,175
5	1940	2,150-2,450
6	1941	2,750-3,150
7	1942	4,050-4,750

Rarity Summary for
Walking Liberty Half Dollars:
1916-1947

OVERALL RARITY IN MINT STATE		
Rank	Issue	Coins Known
1.	1921-S	150-210
2.	1919-S	225-350
3.	1919-D	250-375
4.	1921-D	275-375
5.	1920-D	300-400
6.	1917-S Obv	300-425
7.	1921	325-450
8.	1923-S	375-500
9.	1919	375-525
10.	1920-S	400-500
11.	1917-D Rev	450-550
12.	1928-S	475-600
13.	1916-S	575-700
14.	1918-D	625-725
15.	1917-S Rev	675-775
16.	1927-S	700-800
17.	1918	700-850
18.	1917-D Obv	800-925
19.	1918-S	825-950
20.	1929-S	900-1,075
21.	1920	925-1,050
22.	1929-D	950-1,125
23.	1933-S	975-1,125
24.	1934-S	1,100-1,300
25.	1935-S	1,250-1,475
26.	1916	1,450-1,725
27.	1916-D	1,600-1,850
28.	1935-D	1,650-1,850
29.	1936-S	2,150-2,475
30.	1934-D	2,125-2,525
31.	1937-D	2,185-2,485
32.	1938-D	2,300-2,600
33.	1937-S	2,335-2,635
34.	1917	2,450-2,850

Rarity Summary for
Walking Liberty Half Dollars:
1916-1947 Cont.

OVERALL RARITY IN MINT STATE		
Rank	Issue	Coins Known
35.	1936-D	3,125-3,625
36. (Tie)	1938	3,500-4,050
36. (Tie)	1939-S	3,500-4,050
38.	1935	3,550-4,100
39.	1934	3,575-4,175
40.	1937	4,850-5,450+
41.	1940-S	5,025-5,900+
42.	1939-D	5,100-5,700+
43.	1936	5,600-6,600+
44.	1939	5,725-6,725+
45.	1940	6,200-7,000+
46.	1942-D	7,150-8,150+
47.	1942-S	8,000-9,200+
48.	1943-D	8,400-9,700+
49.	1943-S	8,750-9,750+
50.	1941-D	9,100-9,800+
51.	1941-S	9,200-9,900
52.	1944-D	10,225-11,825+
53.	1944-S	10,200-11,950+
54.	1946	10,675-21,075+
55.	1947-D	11,000-12,800+
56.	1947	11,600-13,000+
57.	1945-S	12,000-13,900+
58.	1944	12,900-14,300+
59.	1945-D	14,000-16,200+
60.	1946-S	14,600-16,500+
61.	1941	15,250-17,500+
62.	1945	18,000-20,000+
63.	1946-D	20,850-24,250+
64.	1942	21,575-24,575+
65.	1943	22,125-25,125+

Rarity Summary for
Walking Liberty Half Dollars:
1916-1947 Cont.

HIGH-GRADE RARITY, MS-65 OR FINER		
Rank	Issue	Coins Known
1.	1919-D	11-15
2.	1921-S	26-37
3.	1918-D	34-45
4.	1917-D Rev	42-55
5.	1921-D	45-56
6.	1920-D	45-57
7.	1917-S Rev	48-60
8.	1917-S Obv	49-60
9.	1918-S	54-65
10.	1919-S	60-75
11.	1921	64-76
12.	1923-S	70-83
13.	1927-S	71-83
14.	1920-S	70-85
15.	1917-D Obv	75-87
16.	1928-S	78-90
17.	1919	85-135
18.	1920	102-125
19.	1916-S	120-150
20.	1918	135-187
21.	1929-D	255-315
22.	1929-S	250-320
23.	1933-S	290-360
24.	1916-D	305-375
25.	1934-S	330-400
26.	1916	370-440
27.	1935-S	450-525
28.	1917	465-535
29.	1935-D	520-580
30.	1934-D	625-775
31.	1936-S	1,110-1,260
32.	1937-D	1,130-1,280
33.	1938-D	1,175-1,325
34.	1937-S	1,210-1,360

Rarity Summary for
Walking Liberty Half Dollars:
1916-1947 Cont.

HIGH-GRADE RARITY, MS-65 OR FINER		
Rank	Issue	Coins Known
35.	1936-D	1,550-1,800
36.	1935	1,650-1,900
37.	1934	1,725-2,025
38.	1940-S	1,825-2,100
39.	1938	1,950-2,250
40.	1937	2,550-2,850
41.	1939-S	2,625-3,025
42.	1941-S	2,775-3,075
43.	1942-S	2,725-3,275
44.	1944-S	3,000-3,550
45.	1939-D	3,175-3,575
46.	1943-S	3,325-3,625
47.	1936	3,200-3,900
48.	1940	3,800-4,250
49.	1939	3,700-4,400
50.	1942-D	4,500-5,200
51.	1947-D	4,725-5,425
52.	1946	4,775-5,475
53.	1945-S	5,275-5,975
54.	1947	5,400-6,100
55.	1941-D	5,900-6,300
56.	1943-D	5,800-6,800
57.	1944	6,125-6,825
58.	1944-D	6,675-7,675
59.	1945	8,775-9,775
60.	1946-S	8,925-10,125
61.	1945-D	9,275-10,775
62.	1941	9,725-11,225
63.	1942	11,525-13,025
64.	1943	12,350-13,850
65.	1946-D	13,050-15,250

Rarity Summary for Early-Date Walking Liberty Half Dollars: 1916-1933

OVERALL RARITY IN MINT STATE		
Rank	Issue	Coins Known
1.	1921-S	150-210
2.	1919-S	225-350
3.	1919-D	250-375
4.	1921-D	275-375
5.	1920-D	300-400
6.	1917-S Obv	300-425
7.	1921	325-450
8.	1923-S	375-500
9.	1919	375-525
10.	1920-S	400-500
11.	1917-D Rev	450-550
12.	1928-S	475-600
13.	1916-S	575-700
14.	1918-D	625-725
15.	1917-S Rev	675-775
16.	1927-S	700-800
17.	1918	700-850
18.	1917-D Obv	800-925
19.	1918-S	825-950
20.	1929-S	900-1,075
21.	1920	925-1,050
22.	1929-D	950-1,125
23.	1933-S	975-1,125
24.	1916	1,450-1,725
25.	1916-D	1,600-1,850
26.	1917	2,450-2,850

Rarity Summary for Early-Date Walking Liberty Half Dollars: 1916-1933 Cont.

HIGH-GRADE RARITY, MS-65 OR FINER		
Rank	Issue	Coins Known
1.	1919-D	11-15
2.	1921-S	26-37
3.	1918-D	34-45
4.	1917-D Rev	42-55
5.	1921-D	45-56
6.	1920-D	45-57
7.	1917-S Rev	48-60
8.	1917-S Obv	49-60
9.	1918-S	54-65
10.	1919-S	60-75
11.	1921	64-76
12.	1923-S	70-83
13.	1927-S	71-83
14.	1920-S	70-85
15.	1917-D Obv	75-87
16.	1928-S	78-90
17.	1919	85-135
18.	1920	102-125
19.	1916-S	120-150
20.	1918	135-187
21.	1929-D	255-315
22.	1929-S	250-320
23.	1933-S	290-360
24.	1916-D	305-375
25.	1916	370-440
26.	1917	465-535

Rarity Summary for Middle-Date Walking Liberty Half Dollars: 1934-1940

OVERALL RARITY IN MINT STATE		
Rank	Issue	Coins Known
1.	1934-S	1,100-1,300
2.	1935-S	1,250-1,475
3.	1935-D	1,650-1,850
4.	1936-S	2,150-2,475
5.	1934-D	2,125-2,525
6.	1937-D	2,185-2,485
7.	1938-D	2,300-2,600
8.	1937-S	2,335-2,635
9.	1936-D	3,125-3,625
10. (Tie)	1938	3,500-4,050
10. (Tie)	1939-S	3,500-4,050
12.	1935	3,550-4,100
13.	1934	3,575-4,175
14.	1937	4,850-5,450+
15.	1940-S	5,025-5,900+
16.	1939-D	5,100-5,700+
17.	1936	5,600-6,600+
18.	1939	5,725-6,725+
19.	1940	6,200-7,000+

Rarity Summary for Middle-Date Walking Liberty Half Dollars: 1934-1940 Cont.

HIGH-GRADE RARITY, MS-65 OR FINER		
Rank	Issue	Coins Known
1.	1934-S	330-400
2.	1935-S	450-525
3.	1935-D	520-580
4.	1934-D	625-775
5.	1936-S	1,110-1,260
6.	1937-D	1,130-1,280
7.	1938-D	1,175-1,325
8.	1937-S	1,210-1,360
9.	1936-D	1,550-1,800
10.	1935	1,650-1,900
11.	1934	1,725-2,025
12.	1940-S	1,850-2,100
13.	1938	1,950-2,250
14.	1937	2,550-2,850
15.	1939-S	2,625-3,025
16.	1939-D	3,175-3,575
17.	1936	3,200-3,900
18.	1940	3,800-4,250
19.	1939	3,700-4,400

Rarity Summary for Late-Date Walking Liberty Half Dollars: 1941-1947

OVERALL RARITY IN MINT STATE		
Rank	Issue	Coins Known
1.	1942-D	7,150-8,150+
2.	1942-S	8,000-9,200+
3.	1943-D	8,400-9,700+
4.	1943-S	8,750-9,750+
5.	1941-D	9,100-9,800+
6.	1941-S	9,200-9,900
7.	1944-D	10,225-11,825+
8.	1944-S	10,200-11,950+
9.	1946	10,675-12,075+
10.	1947-D	11,000-12,800+
11.	1947	11,600-13,000+
12.	1945-S	12,000-13,900+
13.	1944	12,900-14,300+
14.	1945-D	14,000-16,200+
15.	1946-S	14,600-16,500+
16.	1941	15,250-17,500+
17.	1945	18,000-20,000+
18.	1946-D	20,850-24,250+
19.	1942	21,575-24,575+
20.	1943	22,125-25,125+

Rarity Summary for Late-Date Walking Liberty Half Dollars: 1941-1947 Cont.

HIGH-GRADE RARITY, MS-65 OR FINER		
Rank	Issue	Coins Known
1.	1941-S	2,775-3,075
2.	1942-S	2,725-3,275
3.	1944-S	3,000-3,550
4.	1943-S	3,325-3,625
5.	1942-D	4,500-5,200
6.	1947-D	4,725-5,425
7.	1946	4,775-5,475
8.	1945-S	5,275-5,975
9.	1947	5,400-6,100
10.	1943-D	5,800-6,800
11.	1941-D	5,900-6,300
12.	1944	6,125-6,825
13.	1944-D	6,675-7,675
14.	1945	8,775-9,775
15.	1946-S	8,925-10,125
16.	1945-D	9,275-10,775
17.	1941	9,725-11,225
18.	1942	11,525-13,025
19.	1943	12,350-13,850
20.	1946-D	13,050-15,250

Glossary

About Good: The descriptive term associated with the numeric designation of 3 on the 70-point grading scale for United States coins. The abbreviation for About Good is AG.

About Uncirculated: The descriptive term associated with the numeric designations of 50, 53, 55 and 58 on the 70-point grading scale for United States coins. The abbreviation for About Uncirculated is AU.

American Numismatic Association: Chartered by Congress in 1891, the American Numismatic Association is the leading hobby organization in U.S. numismatics. The American Numismatic Association is often referred to by the abbreviation ANA. It is a non-profit organization.

Brilliant Uncirculated: The descriptive term that corresponds to the MS-60, MS-61 and MS-62 grade levels. Brilliant Uncirculated is abbreviated as BU.

Cameo: Coins that display noticeable contrast between frosty devices/lettering and mirror-finish fields. Both PCGS and NGC use this term as a component of the grade assigned to a proof coin.

Certified: A coin that has been submitted to a third-party grading service and returned to the submitter in a sonically sealed, tamper-evident holder. Coins certified by PCGS and NGC enjoy nearly universal acceptance in the U.S. rare coin market of the early 21st century.

Choice AU: The descriptive term that corresponds to the AU-55 grade level.

Choice Uncirculated / Choice Mint State / Choice BU: Descriptive term that corresponds to the MS-63 and MS-64 grade levels.

Clashmarks: Impressions from the devices, legends or other features from one die into the surface of the opposing die in the press. Clashmarks are imparted when a pair of dies comes together in the absence of an intervening planchet. Once they become part of a die, clashmarks are transferred to the surface of a coin during the striking process.

Cleaning: The use of an abrasive substance or device to alter the surfaces of a coin. Cleaned coins often display numerous scattered hairlines on one or both sides and, as impaired examples, are usually not eligible for certification at the major third-party grading services.

Deep Cameo: A proof coin certified by PCGS that has especially bold field-to-device contrast. The corresponding designation at NGC is Ultra Cameo.

Die Polish Lines: See **Striations**.

Dipped: A coin that has been immersed in a weak acid solution to remove toning from the surfaces. Coins that are dipped also lose the outermost layers of metal, which means that the original mint luster will become less vibrant with each subsequent immersion in the dipping solution.

Eagle: A United States gold coin with a face value of $10.00. Regular-issue Eagles were struck in the U.S. Mint from 1795 through 1933.

Extremely Fine: The descriptive term associated with the numeric designations of 40 and 45 on the 70-point grading scale for United States coins. Abbreviations for Extremely Fine include EF and XF.

Fair: The descriptive term associated with the designation 2 on the 70-point grading scale for United States coins. Fair is sometimes abbreviated as FR.

Fine: The descriptive term associated with the numeric designations of 12 and 15 on the 70-point grading scale for United States coins. Fine is sometimes abbreviated as F.

Gem Uncirculated / Gem Mint State / Gem BU: The descriptive term that corresponds to the MS-65, MS-66, Proof-65 and Proof-66 grade levels. Oftentimes only the word Gem is needed to convey the same meaning.

Good: The descriptive term associated with the numeric designations of 4 and 6 on the 70-point grading scale for United States coins. Good is sometimes abbreviated as G.

Hairlines: Thin lines on a coin's surfaces that, when used in reference to a business strike example, are indicative of cleaning or another form of mishandling. Hairlines are also used to describe light handling marks on proof coins and, in this case, are not always the result of cleaning. Unlike die polish lines, hairlines are set below the surface of a coin.

Half Dollar: A United States coin with a face value of 50 cents. Half Dollars have been struck in the United States Mint since 1794.

Hub: A master die from which working dies are created.

Impaired: A descriptive term for coins that have been cleaned, damaged, whizzed, repaired or otherwise mishandled to the point where they will trade at a discounted price. It is the stated policy of major third-party grading services such as PCGS and NGC that impaired coins are not eligible for certification and will be returned to the submitter without being mounted in a plastic holder.

Insert: The small piece of paper included in the holder with coins certified by PCGS, NGC and other third-party grading services. Upon the insert are found such important information as the coin's date, denomination, grade and, if applicable, variety.

Luster: The original finish imparted to a coin at the time of striking. Or, the amount and intensity of light reflected from a coin's surface.

Mint State: A coin struck for circulation but that does not display any evidence of wear. Mint State coins are graded on a numeric scale from 60-70. The term Uncirculated also describes a Mint State coin.

Near-Gem: The descriptive term that corresponds to the MS-64 and Proof-64 grade levels.

Near-Mint: The descriptive term that corresponds to the AU-58 grade level.

NGC Census: A listing of all coins certified by NGC. Up-to-date versions of the NGC Census are available for free viewing through the firm's website, www.ngccoin.com.

Numismatic Guaranty Corporation: Founded in 1987, NGC authenticates, grades and encapsulates coins for a fee. Along with PCGS, it is the leading third-party certification service in the U.S. rare coin market of the early 21st century.

Numismatics: The study or collection of rare coins. A person who studies, collects or invests in rare coins is known as a numismatist.

PCGS Population Report: A listing of all coins certified by PCGS. Up-to-date versions of the PCGS Population Report are accessible for a fee through the firm's website, www.pcgs.com.

Polishing: An especially severe form of cleaning. Coins that have been polished display unnaturally bright and/or glossy-textured surfaces. Technically impaired, polished coins are not eligible for certification at the major third-party grading services.

Poor: The descriptive term associated with the numeric designation of 1 on the 70-point grading scale for United States coins. Poor is sometimes abbreviated as PO.

Prime Focal Areas: The most important surface areas of a coin when evaluating eye appeal and/or technical grade. Examples of prime focal areas are Liberty's cheek, the date and the mintmark. Abrasions or other distractions in prime focal areas will have a more profound effect on a coin's eye appeal than if they were located in a less-critical area.

Professional Coin Grading Service: Founded in 1986, PCGS authenticates, grades and encapsulates coins for a fee. Along with NGC, it is the leading third-party certification service in the U.S. rare coin market of the early 21st century.

Professional Numismatists Guild: An organization of rare coin and paper money experts whose members are held to high standards of integrity and professionalism. The abbreviation for the Professional Numismatists Guild is PNG. It is a non-profit organization.

Resubmissions: A term that professional numismatists use to describe coins that are removed from PCGS and NGC holders and submitted to these services at least one more time in the hopes of securing a higher grade. Resubmissions skew the number of coins listed in the PCGS Population Report and NGC Census when the submitter has not returned the old insert(s) to the grading services.

Striations: Incuse lines on the surface of a die that result from polishing during the preparation process. When transferred to a coin during striking, striations will appear as raised lines. Since these features are as struck, striations will not result in a lower numeric grade from PCGS or NGC.

Superb Gem: The descriptive term that corresponds to the MS-67, MS-68, MS-69, Proof-67, Proof-68 and Proof-69 grade levels.

Toning: The color or colors seen on one or both sides of many coins. The intensity and variety of toning that a coin displays is a function of how, where and how long it was stored.

Very Fine: The descriptive term associated with the numeric designations of 20, 25, 30 and 35 on the 70-point grading scale for United States coins. The abbreviation for Very Fine is VF.

Very Good: The descriptive term associated with the numeric designations of 8 and 10 on the 70-point grading scale for United States coins. The abbreviation for Very Good is VG.

Whizzing: An attempt to simulate original luster on a coin's surface through the use of a wire brush or similar device. Whizzed coins are considered to be impaired and are not eligible for certification at the major third-party grading services.

Bibliography

Bowers and Merena Auctions. http://www.bowersandmerena.com/. Prices realized archives, various sales, accessed October-November, 2007.

Breen, Walter. *Walter Breen's Complete Encyclopedia of U.S. and Colonial Coins.* New York, New York: Doubleday, 1988.

Burdette, Roger W. *Renaissance of American Coinage: 1916-1921.* Great Falls, Virginia: Seneca Mills Press, 2005.

Coin Dealer Newsletter, The. *The Coin Dealer Newsletter, Vol. XLV, No. 44.* Torrance, California, November 2, 2007.

Coin Dealer Newsletter, The. *The Coin Dealer Newsletter Monthly Supplement, Vol. XXXII, No. 10.* Torrance, California: October 12, 2007.

Dannreuther, John and Garrett, Jeff. *The Official Red Book of Auction Records: 1995-2004, U.S. Small Cents-Silver Dollars.* Atlanta, Georgia: Whitman Publishing, LLC, 2005.

David Lawrence Rare Coins. http://www.davidlawrence.com/. Prices realized archives, Richmond Collection Part II, accessed October-November, 2007.

Fivaz, Bill and Stanton, J. T. *Cherrypickers' Guide to Rare Die Varieties of United States Coins*, Fourth Edition, Volume II. Atlanta, Georgia, Whitman Publishing, LLC, 2006.

Fox, Bruce. *The Complete Guide to Walking Liberty Half Dollars.* Virginia Beach, Virginia: DLRC Press, 1993.

Heritage Auction Galleries. http://coins.ha.com/default.php. Prices realized archives, various sales, accessed October-November, 2007.

Ira & Larry Goldberg Auctioneers. http://www.goldbergcoins.com/index.shtml. Prices realized archives, various sales, accessed October-November, 2007.

Numismatic Guaranty Corporation. Online Population Report. http://www.ngccoin.com/. Accessed October-November, 2007.

Professional Coin Grading Service. *Official Guide to Coin Grading and Counterfeit Detection.* New York, New York: House of Collectibles, 1997.

Professional Coin Grading Service. *PCGS Population Report.* http://www.pcgs.com/. Accessed October-November, 2007.

Stack's. http://www.stacks.com/. Prices realized archives, various sales, accessed October-November, 2007.

Stanford Coins & Bullion, Inc. *Auction Values.* http://www.ecoinage.com/. Prices realized archives, various 20th century U.S. gold coin issues, accessed October-November, 2007.

Superior Galleries. http://www.sgbh.com/Shop/home/index.html. Prices realized archives, various U.S. gold coin issues, accessed October-November, 2007.

Wikipedia. http://en.wikipedia.org/wiki/Main_Page. Biographical information on Adolph Alexander Weinman at http://en.wikipedia.org/wiki/Adolph_Alexander_ Weinman, accessed January, 2008.

Yeoman, R. S. *A Guide Book of United States Coins*, 61ˢᵗ Edition. Atlanta, Georgia: Whitman Publishing, LLC, 2007.